WORLD BANK TECHNICAL PAPER NO. 488

Governance Impact on Private Investment

Evidence from the International Patterns of Infrastructure Bond Risk Pricing

D1530298

Nina B. Bubnova

The World Bank
Washington, D.C.

Copyright © 2000
The International Bank for Reconstruction
and Development/THE WORLD BANK
1818 H Street, N.W.
Washington, D.C. 20433, U.S.A.

All rights reserved
Manufactured in the United States of America
First printing August 2000
1 2 3 4 04 03 02 01 00

Technical Papers are published to communicate the results of the Bank's work to the development community with the least possible delay. The typescript of this paper therefore has not been prepared in accordance with the procedures appropriate to formal printed texts, and the World Bank accepts no responsibility for errors. Some sources cited in this paper may be informal documents that are not readily available.

The findings, interpretations, and conclusions expressed in this paper are entirely those of the author(s) and should not be attributed in any manner to the World Bank, to its affiliated organizations, or to members of its Board of Executive Directors or the countries they represent. The World Bank does not guarantee the accuracy of the data included in this publication and accepts no responsibility for any consequence of their use. The boundaries, colors, denominations, and other information shown on any map in this volume do not imply on the part of the World Bank Group any judgment on the legal status of any territory or the endorsement or acceptance of such boundaries.

The material in this publication is copyrighted. The World Bank encourages dissemination of its work and will normally grant permission promptly.

Permission to photocopy items for internal or personal use, for the internal or personal use of specific clients, or for educational classroom use, is granted by the World Bank, provided that the appropriate fee is paid directly to Copyright Clearance Center, Inc., 222 Rosewood Drive, Danvers, MA 01923, U.S.A., telephone 978-750-8400, fax 978-750-4470. Please contact the Copyright Clearance Center before photocopying items.

For permission to reprint individual articles or chapters, please fax your request with complete information to the Republication Department, Copyright Clearance Center, fax 978-750-4470.

All other queries on rights and licenses should be addressed to the World Bank at the address above or faxed to 202-522-2422.

ISBN: 0-8213-4818-3
ISSN: 0253-7494

Nina B. Bubnova is a consultant for the energy sector unit of the Europe and Central Asia Region of the World Bank.

Library of Congress Cataloging-in-Publication Data has been applied for.

Contents

iii

Figures

Tables

Annex Tables

Foreword

The Energy Department of the World Bank's Europe and Central Asia Region has been undertaking analytical work on issues pertinent to the Bank-wide effort to confine corruption and strengthen governance frameworks in member countries in order to foster economic development, the provision of essential infrastructure services, and the expansion of private investment.

This research is a step toward a better understanding of the nature of governance frameworks, the risks they place on private investment, and the barriers they raise to infrastructure development. The findings of this research are valuable both for public and private sector actors: assisting the former in the design of public policies aimed at the creation of attractive investment environments; and assisting the latter in making the appropriate strategic choices when entering infrastructure investment business transactions.

Hossein Razavi
Director
Energy Department
Europe and Central Asia Region

Acknowledgements

The author would like to express her gratitude to Messrs. Hossein Razavi, Director, and Laszlo Lovei, Lead Energy Specialist, Energy Department, ECA, for launching this research on the impact of governance in infrastructure finance and for their support during the project. Special thanks go to Ms. Jenifer Wishart and Messrs. Robert Bacon, Gregory Ingram, Eugene Gurenko, Philip Keefer, Michael Klein, Guy Pfefferman, Warrick Smith, Pablo Spiller, John Quigley, Oliver Williamson, and seminar participants at UC Berkeley for their comments on previous versions. The author is grateful to Mr. Ilya Lipkovich, Virginia Polytechnical School, for his advice on the application of modern statistical theory to the analysis of the research. Funding for this research was generously provided by the grant of the Research Committee of the World Bank and by the Award of the Graduate Chancellor of the University of California, Berkeley.

Nina B. Bubnova
University of California, Berkeley

Abstract

During the last decade, infrastructure finance and provision graduated from traditional means to more innovative ones, primarily initiated by private companies and supported through their equity and debt. Capital markets increasingly became the main funding source for infrastructure projects worldwide, including investments in developing and transition countries where infrastructure penetration still falls considerably short of needs. Infrastructure bonds served as the most popular method of oil, gas, electricity, telecommunications, and transport project financing in these countries throughout 1990–99, thereby substituting government funding.

Thriving markets require not only an appropriately designed economic system, but also a secure political foundation that limits the ability of the state to confiscate wealth. This requires a presence of political institutions that credibly commit the state to honor economic and political rights. Investments in infrastructure are particularly susceptible to the risks of government interference. Constructive government noninvolvement—necessary regulation excepted—is likely to fail in societies that lack the institutions to serve as checks and balances on government action, as well as in those societies that do not possess a longstanding tradition of law and order. These and other risks impinge on investor confidence, an effect exacerbated by the recent global financial crisis. The need to boost private capital flow to infrastructure projects requires policy measures that will reduce investor perceptions of the risk of default due to adverse government action.

This paper uses international cross-sectional and time-series infrastructure bond risk premium and credit rating history data from the past decade to examine the factors that influence investor risk perceptions and that inflate the cost of borrowing for essential infrastructure. The information thus generated about key governance risks is then analyzed for its policy implications.

Executive Summary

Prior to the late 1980s, funds for long-term infrastructure investments in most emerging economies were provided only by or through government. Fiscal austerity measures and other factors have since caused most governments to cut their budgetary contributions to infrastructure, and private sector funding has emerged as a substitute for government funding. In accordance with the common practice of infrastructure finance in the industrialized world, bonds in particular have become a major conduit of private capital flow to infrastructure projects in emerging markets. The rapid growth of private capital investment has however been insufficient to satisfy market demand in these countries: an estimated 3.5 billion people worldwide do not have access to basic infrastructure services today.[1]

One way to encourage greater private investment in infrastructure development is to reduce investor risk. In addition to macroeconomic, capital market, and firm-intrinsic factors, the likelihood of infrastructure bond default is increased by nontransparent and unpredictable regulatory frameworks, weak systems of contract enforcement, and the lack of political stability. These factors are particularly significant because infrastructure investments are typically large, long-term, and irreversible, and because they are dependent on sales to domestic markets and on government regulatory intervention, which may include the setting of prices and quality standards. Such risks have not been taken into account in previous empirical analysis of private lending to infrastructure sectors.

This research paper aims to contribute to our existing knowledge by providing a thorough examination of the effect that governance frameworks, both political and regulatory, have on investors' risk perceptions and on associated costs. It aims to achieve this by analyzing the rich cross-sectional data and time-series data generated by the universe of fixed-rate infrastructure bonds issued and traded during the past decade. The research considered such polity and governance aspects as the historical enforcement of the law, including the extent of regulatory discretion and the political constraints on that discretion; the presence of corruption; the quality of bureaucracy; the ability of the system to enforce adherence to contracts; and the likelihood of expropriation and other political risks. It additionally identified those political and regulatory risks that most concern investors. While most previous research has focused separately on the cases of the developing and industrialized worlds, this paper provides a comparative analysis of developed and emerging infrastructure bond markets. This enables us to see how the factors that drive infrastructure finance in the two country groups differ, and thereby enables us to identify the policy implications of these differences.

The methodological approach used is innovative in five areas: (1) it enhances the explanatory capacity of earlier credit risk models by combining firm-intrinsic and macroeconomic factors and by adding the full spectrum of risks associated with the quality of governance and regulation in a country and sector of bond issuance; (2) it applies hierarchical cluster analysis to understand an array of current regulatory and political risk indicators and to discern the variables that drive the governance risk perception in a given country; (3) it complements analysis based on cross-sectional data by constructing a database of time-series yield data on infrastructure bonds traded in the secondary market and by examining the factors that affect bond risk in real market conditions; (4) it investigates the role of industry structure and regulation as applied to the power sector segment of infrastructure bonds; and (5) it compiles and analyzes the rating history of the entire bonds universe and uses the history of upgrade and downgrade events to investigate the impact of governance over the lifetime of an infrastructure bond. The research utilized the techniques of principal component analysis and cluster analysis; ordinary least squares analysis and two staged least squares with instrumental variables regression analysis; truncated and augmented regression analysis; and multinomial logit regression analysis.

The research yielded five related, yet distinct conclusions.

First, it confirmed the hypothesis that governance risk has a strong impact on the perceived default risk of a fixed income security, although the effects of the various political and regulatory risks on bond spreads are clearly not homogeneous. Cluster analysis segregated an array of 19 regulatory and political risk indicators into four risk groups: (1) political disorder; (2) corruption, red tape, and autocracy; (3) poor economic policy; and (4) fundamentalism.

Empirical evidence suggests that what matters most to investors are the risks of corruption, the poor quality of the bureaucracy, and the lack of institutional constraints on governmental action. As estimated by this research, governance-borne risks in emerging bond markets, calculated as payments that could have been avoided, cost investors about $677.7 million in 1997. (Note that dollar amounts in this paper are U.S. unless otherwise indicated.)

These risks, classified here as corruption, red tape, and autocracy risks, are followed in importance by the traditional risks of political disorder caused by civil war, by the involvement in politics of the military, by political terrorism, by the lack of adequate law enforcement, and by nationalization policies. Investors appear to be least concerned by risks that stem from short-sighted economic policies and poor planning, as well as by so-called fundamentalism risks that are associated with the prevalence of organized religion in politics, with internal racial and nationality tensions, and with the risk of external conflict.

In other words, investors are able through diversification to discount some incompetence in political and economic leadership and some erratic economic policies. Empirically, it appears that poor political leadership and economic mismanagement are now seen as diversifiable incompetence and no longer constitute a systemic threat to investors. But while investors can similarly make allowances for differences in the cultural and moral endowments of a country, they cannot discount the hazards that stem from systemic incentives to steal (corruption) or to break commitments (poor contract enforceability), which reduce expected values and require an offsetting spread.

These findings on the hierarchical importance of the four risk clusters were reinforced by results of the time-series examination of bond credit risk structure in the secondary market, with the only difference being that all four governance risk clusters had a significant effect on the secondary market spread. Spreads in the aftermarket essentially measure the monetary compensation for the risk of bond default, as dictated by real market risk judgement, as opposed to bond spreads at-issuance, which are determined by associated risk judgement by analysts at the underwriting banks and at the institutional investment entities.

Second, the research identified a clear separation of the sample universe of countries into three regulatory and political risk clusters, defined as those with stable, weak, and risky governance climates. These groups to a large extent correspond to what the development community conventionally calls the "industrialized," "emerging," and "developing" worlds. Members of the "risky" governance cluster[2]—the least developed countries and the stumbling transition economies—generally have very poor governance and poor macroeconomic indicators, and have to pay high premiums to investors for taking on the risk. Countries from the "weak" cluster—the emerging economies[3]—have some of the fundamentals in place, such as appropriate fiscal and monetary policies and ownership structures, but face governance issues, particularly those that give rise to political and regulatory risks, as their toughest challenge. The "stable" or industrialized countries[4] are in the clear, with the risk premiums of bonds issued in these countries found to be unaffected by governance risks. Investors in the stable cluster countries can focus on real commercial project risks rather than on policy risks created by potentially adverse government actions. A noteworthy conclusion to be drawn from this finding is that economic reform remains a necessary but not a sufficient approach to development.

As a case study, the research applied the model developed here to estimate the expected risk return for infrastructure investors in two transition economies, the Czech Republic and Hungary, in 1997. The Czech Republic notably issued more infrastructure bonds than any other Central and Eastern European country; Hungary, in contrast, preferred other types of infrastructure financing. The model estimation indicated that the cost of borrowing in Hungary should be higher and in the Czech Republic lower than the actual average spread for emerging market countries in that year, in order to compensate potential investors for the political and regulatory risks that they would face. This may partly explain the difference in the two countries' choices of infrastructure finance sources.

Third, the research found a substantial degree of variation in the impact of regulatory and political risks on the spread for bond issuers, according to their institutional and ownership characteristics. There is clear evidence of asymmetry in the degree of exposure to adverse government action that bond issuers face, dependent on their ownership status. Specifically, private sector infrastructure projects were found to be more vulnerable to the effect of political and regulatory risks than were public projects. Simultaneously, public ownership of an infrastructure project was found to set the influence of firm-intrinsic factors on the bond spread to zero, suggesting that questions of the economic efficiency and financial prudence of public companies are not taken into account when the risk of their infrastructure projects is evaluated. In reality, the business weaknesses of public companies tend to be compensated for by the ability of governments to cross-subsidize those companies and to apply favorable tax breaks.

This research further studies the effects internationally of risks posed by industry structure and regulation. By examining the risk premium structure of bonds issued for the financing of power sector projects, the research established that there is a fine line between the benefits that accrue from the granting of regulatory independence and the hazards, as perceived by investors, that potentially stem from giving discretionary powers to the price regulator. Specifically, the research found that the absence of institutional constraints on the ability of regulators to set prices significantly increases the investment risk, as measured by the bond spread. Low levels of power sector privatization were similarly found to increase investor perceptions of risk.

Finally, a study of the credit rating history of the sample universe of bonds enabled an examination of the factors underlying investment's creditworthiness stability and creditworthiness change. This indicated that stable governance frameworks are essential for a stable credit rating history, and that changes in firm-intrinsic characteristics are instrumental in causing the upgrade or downgrade of a bond by the major credit rating agencies.

1. Introduction

Fueled by fiscal constraints and growing disenchantment with the performance of state-provided infrastructure services, the trend of liberalizing and privatizing infrastructure services that began in the late 1970s and 1980s turned into a wave that swept the world in the 1990s (World Bank, 1999). Recognizing the ability of the private sector to provide cost-effective, high-quality solutions for the delivery of essential utility services, more and more governments turned to private sources for the financing and provision of telecommunications, energy, transport, and water services. Even the traditionally state-ownership-oriented developing countries experienced a growth in private activity in infrastructure. Investment in infrastructure projects with private participation grew dramatically from about US$16 billion annually to US$120 billion[5] in 1990–97; although it declined by about one-fifth to US$95 billion in 1998, as a repercussion of the financial crisis that began in Asia, the World Bank estimates that the private sector today contributes about 40 percent of the total infrastructure investment in developing countries.

Increasingly, it is private capital rather than public expenditures that has funded infrastructure projects and firms. In accordance with the common practice of infrastructure finance in the industrialized world, bonds in particular became a major conduit of private capital flow to infrastructure projects in emerging markets in the 1990s. Despite its rapid growth, however, the extent of private capital investment in these markets has been insufficient to satisfy demand: an estimated 3.5 billion people worldwide still do not have access to basic infrastructure services.[6]

The flow of private investment is extremely sensitive to political hazards associated with the unpredictability of future government actions. This problem is particularly acute in infrastructure development, because infrastructure investments are typically large, long-term, and irreversible, and they are usually dependent on sales to domestic markets. Government involvement is also heavier in these sectors, as manifested in the regulation of entry prices and in quality and environmental standards. Infrastructure services are additionally often essential to the consumer, but are frequently provided by monopolists. Together, these factors increase political sensitivity to the prices charged. Pressure from consumers to keep prices low makes it politically difficult for governments to maintain prices that cover costs. Regulatory risks, defined as those risks arising from the application and enforcement of regulatory rules, both at the economy-wide and at the industry- or project-specific level, including rules contained in contracts with governments, in laws, and in other regulatory instruments, can deter investors, increase the cost of investment capital, increase required tariffs, and/or reduce the proceeds from privatization. In addition, infrastructure projects typically require large sunk investments that may take 10 to 30 years to recoup. Over such long periods of time investors are exposed to serious risks, in particular the risk that public authori-

1

ties will not honor their agreements on tariff policy and payments to investors. Once investors are committed to a project and able to pull out only by taking on a huge loss, the government may be tempted to exercise administrative expropriation through lowering prices or not raising them as agreed. One consequence of the 1997 financial crisis in developing countries in fact has been the deterioration of demand for and supply of private infrastructure, with many high-level projects cancelled and growth forecasts for developing countries revised downward. Regulatory risks such as these are further supplemented by broader-based macro-level political risks associated with poor governance and inadequate enforcement of law and order. Such risks include the familiar political risks of expropriation and nationalization, the uncertainty that stems from weak systems of contract enforcement and the absence of an independent judiciary, corruption, and poor bureaucratic quality.

These problems together discourage potential investors from investing in environments that lack credible government commitment. However, it is not always clear what investors are looking for and what—apart from sustainable macroeconomic and ownership structure reforms—should therefore be the preconditions to encourage private investment and the successful privatization of infrastructure services. This paper uses the yield spread as a measure of credit risk to investigate the effects of various aspects of governance—including the presence of corruption, quality of the bureaucracy, contract enforceability, law and order tradition, expropriation, and other risks—on the perception of bond default risk. Of these, it seeks to identify those factors that most concern investors. The paper also seeks to enhance the explanatory capacity of earlier credit risk models by considering the full spectrum of independent variables: firm- and bond-intrinsic characteristics, macroeconomic factors, and the range of risks associated with the quality of governance and regulation in a country and sector of bond issue. The impact of regulatory risks is further investigated by examination of time-series data on spreads of those infrastructure bonds that were traded in the aftermarket.

The paper is organized into eight sections. Section 2 discusses prior research in this area. Section 3 elaborates the conceptual framework of the proposed study and Section 4 describes the data employed. Section 5 describes the results of the regulatory risk data cluster analysis and examines what drives governance risk perception. Section 6 discusses the use of cross-sectional at-issuance risk premium data to assess the impact of (1) macro-level and (2) industry-level regulatory risks on finance cost at investor entry, and further applies the model thus developed to study the impact of macro-level regulatory risks on infrastructure finance in Hungary. Section 7 utilizes time-series data on the life of infrastructure bonds in the secondary market to (1) identify what risks are significant in "real" market conditions and to (2) assess how political and regulatory risks contribute to the likelihood of positive or negative changes in a bond's credit rating history. Section 8 concludes the paper. Detailed descriptions of the applied models and estimation techniques used here are presented in five Methodological Appendixes at the end of the paper.

2. Previous Research

The literature devoted to credit risk measurement can be divided into three broad categories. The first looks exclusively at firm-intrinsic determinants of credit risk and premium, and includes works by Hoboken (1991), Altman and others (1997), and others. As described earlier, this approach is based on analysis of bond issuer business fundamentals, including financial statements, profitability, liquidity, and capital structure. The second category looks at capital markets and firm determinants, particularly the level and volatility of company share prices, and is represented by Beaver (1968), Merton (1973), and Fama and French (1993).

The third category, and the one within which this paper primarily belongs, is dedicated to the macroeconomic and institutional determinants of credit risk and investment flows. Theoretical discussion of the economic impact of political institutions has expanded dramatically since North and Thomas (1973) first outlined a "transaction cost view of economic history." Acceptance of the crucial role that sociopolitical structures play in reducing the cost of contracts and in bargaining, monitoring, and enforcement has achieved the status of conventional wisdom, not only among economic historians such as North (1990), but also among economic development theorists such as Borner, Brunetti, and Weder (1995), Olson (1996), and the World Bank (1997). Political forces have the potential to intervene and halt the development of a market system or to redistribute the wealth thus created. As noted by Weingast (1993), not only do political forces hold the potential to destroy a fragile, nascent economic system; the fear that that power will be exercised also deters the economic activity necessary for economic growth. The absence of secure protection of the reward for effort deters investment and hence economic development (North (1990), Olson (1996), Williamson (1991)). The fundamental policy question is therefore what form of political and regulatory systems are required to ensure that a viable, stable private market economy is produced by these systems? The answer offered by the school of new institutional economics envisages the creation of political institutions that enforce governments to credibly commit to noninterference with private property. Such institutions are instrumental to the successful promotion of economic growth and the facilitation and participation of private investment (Levy and Spiller (1994), North (1993), Williamson (1991)).

In addition to this conceptual research, work has also been done to understand on an empirical level the relationship between governance and regulation and private investment in infrastructure. A number of research works appeared in the 1980s, when the finance community in the United States became interested in the impact of Public Utility Commission regulations on the risks associated with investments in U.S. utilities. Analysis of utility bond ratings and rankings assigned to the U.S. state utility commissions by U.S. investment advisory services identified several factors that were suggested to be instrumental in explaining the greater risk associated with investment in utilities firms (Chandrasekaran and Dukes

(1981), Davidson and Chandy (1983), and Navarro (1983)). These factors included the utility firm's beta, regulatory lag, interest rates, the rate of return on equity, the election or appointment of a utility commissioner, the existence of an option to pass on the cost of fuel adjustment to the customer, and an allowance in the rate base for construction work in progress.

Valuable evidence of the investment incentives that state regulation can provide is also available in the literature of public finance, in the form of analysis of the effect of state fiscal institutions such as balanced budget rules and restrictions on state debt issuance on the yields of state general obligation bonds. Poterba and Rueben (1997) find that states with tighter anti-deficit rules and more restrictive provisions on state debt issuance pay lower interest rates on their bonds. Other authors, including Eichengreen (1992), Goldstein and Woglom (1992), Bayoumi and others (1995), and Lowry and Alt (1997) also find a correlation between fiscal regulations in the U.S. states and the interest rate on the bonds issued by these states. This evidence suggests that bond market participants in industrialized countries consider fiscal regulations when assessing the risk associated with state bond issues, which if true might have important implications for emerging market economies. For example, in Ukraine, strict municipal expenditure rules encourage timely payments to their local utilities by those budgetary customers that are subsidized from the municipal budget; this helps maintain a reliable cash flow and assures timely payments to the potential investor.

The existing literature of the developing countries tends to limit explanation of private capital flow to one or two sets of independent variables, such as macroeconomic factors (Hajivassiliou, 1989), exchange and interest rate risk (Masuoka, 1990), and macroeconomic and project-specific variables (Dailami and Leipziger, 1997). An important exception is the dissertation work by Henisz (1996), who developed a measure of political constraints that protect investors from governmental discretion. Henisz forged an explicit link between this measure and variations in cross-national growth rates and the volume of infrastructure investment.

There have been a number of systematic studies of the cost of capital raised through bond issues in developing countries. A detailed analysis of credit risk premiums was done by Edwards (1986), who empirically studied the pricing of bonds and loans in international markets. The focus of this work, however, is limited to the risk premiums of sovereign bonds and loans to developing countries, and to macroeconomic independent variables such as the ratios of debt to GNP, reserves to GNP, gross investment to GNP, and debt service to exports, as well as to growth indicators, maturity, and principal of the bond. While Edwards' paper identifies the significant effect of debt ratios on risk premium, it takes no account of governance risk indicators. Cantor and Packer (1996) analyzed the determinants of spreads on sovereign bonds for 49 countries in 1995, relating spreads to macroeconomic factors, default history, and to Standard and Poor's and Moody's country credit ratings. The limitations of this study, as identified in Eichengreen and Mody (1998), include the fact that it analyzes only sovereign bonds. Cline (1995) limits his study to cases of highly indebted countries and considers only four macroeconomic determinants of interest rate spreads. A 1997 follow-up study by Cline and Barnes uses more recent data and a longer list of explanatory variables, but otherwise is subject to the same limitations. Eichengreen and Portes (1989) analyze a larger sample of bonds issued in the 1920s; however, the debt pricing patterns could have changed over time. A similar concern attaches to Edwards' 1986 study of bond spreads on 167 issues for 13 countries in 1976–80. Finally, Eichengreen and Mody (1998) studied the spreads on 863 bonds issued in developing countries from 1991 through 1995, relating those spreads to bond characteristics, country macroeconomic factors, and global economic conditions. As in other studies, the potential significance of political and regulatory risks was not considered. The study was additionally limited to Latin America and East Asia, and excluded examination of Eastern European bond issues.

The objective of this paper is to fill in these gaps and to help achieve an understanding of what governance features are instrumental for stable private investment and participation in infrastructure. To evaluate the influence of the described risk factors on the cost of debt capital in infrastructure projects, the determinants of bond spreads, defined as a risk premium over a U.S Treasury benchmark rate, are analyzed. The research considers the entire universe of bond issues, covering more than 40 developing and industrialized countries, and the entire universe of potentially significant factors—macroeconomic, financial, political, and regulatory—that are hypothetically related to the risk of bond default.

3. Analytical Framework

To evaluate the influence of the previously described risk factors on the cost of debt capital in infrastructure projects, the determinants of bond spreads (defined as a risk premium over a benchmark rate set by riskless U.S. Treasury bonds) are analyzed for the universe of fixed-rate infrastructure bonds issued during the last decade. A fixed-income security investment decision is based on the relative value of the bond. One of the main factors in assessing this value is the risk of bond default. Investors are compensated for such risk by a risk premium, or spread, on bond yield.[7] The spread is a dependent variable, with investors requiring a higher spread when investing in riskier assets in order to cover the expected loss from potential default.

Credit analysts and researchers employ three main analytical methodologies to analyze credit risk: (1) the firm-intrinsic approach, (2) the firm-capital market approach, and (3) the firm-macroeconomic approach (as reviewed in Altman and Saunders, 1997).

A firm-intrinsic credit model is based on specific information about the issuing firm's fundamentals, including its financial statements, profitability, liquidity, and capital structure. A composite effect of these indicators is used to measure the extent of corporate default vulnerability. Although a firm-intrinsic model enables the direct comparison of an individual company with other companies that may have compromised their creditors, it does not account for capital market effects or for the global and local economic and governance conditions that also impact the probability of bond issuer default.

Firm-capital market models rely almost exclusively on capital market movement information to assess the financial vulnerability of issuer firms. The key information used by these models is the level and volatility of the company's stock price, which has been proven to be a helpful indicator of a firm's financial health. The resulting measure of a firm's creditworthiness nonetheless remains a rather volatile indicator.

In contrast to the firm-capital model, which takes security valuation notions as its explanatory variables, the third approach employs macroeconomic factors. The firm-macroeconomic methodology analyzes the impact of variables such as economic growth, inflation, interest rates, and capital market activity on a firm's ability to sustain its financial obligations.

Each of these approaches to credit risk estimation provides only partial understanding of the problem. In some cases they do not account for firm and capital market characteristics; in others, they do not factor in macroeconomic indicators. None of them takes account of the governance characteristics of the country and sector of bond issuance. This implies that these models, neither separately nor in combination, are sufficient to understand the determinants of credit risk in emerging markets characterized by volatile political and macroeconomic conditions.

This research develops a simple framework to understand the role that country governance and industry regulation play in the formulation of investor risk perceptions and in the determination of the cost of infrastructure bond financing. It seeks to find an answer to the following questions:

1. What governance, political, and regulatory risks impact the cost of private debt capital for infrastructure projects? Which of these risks do investors perceive as diversifiable and which as irreversible?
2. What is the aggregate weight of individual and combined regulatory risks and how does their impact compare with that of other factors in governing risk premiums on private bond debt finance for infrastructure?
3. Which countries do potential investors perceive as being of the greatest risk? What are the institutional characteristics that prevent these countries from being classified as investment grade?
4. Are bond at-issuance risk premiums driven by analyst risk perceptions or by true market conditions? Is the structure of the bond spread at-issuance systemically different from that in the aftermarket?
5. How do governance factors affect bond risk pricing over the lifetime of the bond? Do changes in political and regulatory conditions matter in bond downgrades?

To address these questions, this research analyzes a rich set of cross-sectional and time-series data on bond spreads and on the corresponding macroeconomic, governance, and bond financial characteristics. It uses the techniques of cluster (principal component) analysis, simple ordinary least squares, and two-stage least squares, and applies the random correlation effects model and ordered and multinomial logit regressions.

Dependent Variables

Bonds are appropriate as the subject of analysis as they have become since the 1990s a major conduit of private capital flow to infrastructure projects in emerging markets. The basic value of a bond rests on the investor's assessment of the relative attractiveness of the expected stream of future interest receipts and the prospect of eventual recovery of the principal at maturity. Investors consider the risks underlying the bond contract in terms of the issuing company's future ability to generate sufficient cash with which to repay both interest and principal. The collective judgement of investors about the issuing company's ability to do this will influence both the price level at which the bond is publicly traded and the particular risk category accorded to the bond. Investors expect to earn a higher spread when investing in riskier assets to compensate for taking the extra risk.

To evaluate the influence of the above factors on the cost of debt capital in emerging economies, we must analyze the determinants of bond yield spreads, defined as a risk premium over a benchmark rate (that is, of a U.S. Treasury bond of the same maturity). The bond spread is measured by taking the difference between the annual yield of the considered bond and the annual yield of a U.S. Treasury bond of the same maturity on the date of bond issuance. To understand bond risk pricing in real market conditions, time-series analysis uses secondary market bond spreads, as determined by the difference between the annual yield of the considered bond and the annual yield of a U.S. Treasury bond of the same maturity on the date of secondary market transaction.

Independent Variables

Throughout this analysis, the research will employ the following exogenous risk factors:

- Macroeconomic risk indicators—that is, a country's economic creditworthiness and propensity to default factors.
- Bond issue and issuer characteristics—that is, firm-intrinsic and/or bond-intrinsic characteristics accounting for the firm's and project's financial sustainability and the issuer's creditworthiness.
- Regulatory and political risks—that is, economy-wide measures of governance stability and credibility.

Macroeconomic factors increasing the probability of default have traditionally been included in the analysis of investment trends and of the determinants of the cost of debt capital. In analyzing a country's business environment, investors assess the likelihood of change in economic conditions, which could impact the market demand and the price of project output; the cost of project inputs, including labor costs; and the foreign exchange rate. Earlier studies have found that high private sector investment rates are associated with high domestic production and demand growth and low inflation, low fiscal deficits, and low external indebtedness. This research accounts for the influence of the following macroeconomic factors as determinants of the cost of debt capital for infrastructure projects: (1) real GDP per capita, adjusted for inflation; (2) annual GDP growth rate; (3) the volume of foreign direct investment, as a percentage of GDP; and (4) the volume of stocks traded, as a percentage of GDP.

High national levels of real GDP per capita, GDP growth, and current revenues are normally signs of an overall stable macroeconomic environment, and they therefore enhance the creditworthiness of bond issuers in such a country. The volume of foreign direct investment as a percentage of GDP serves as an indicator of the attractiveness of the local economy to investment from abroad, and high levels of foreign direct investment can in turn potentially make bond issuance more likely and the spread lower. The volume of stocks traded as a percentage of GDP and the amount of private, nonguaranteed debt signify the level of financial market development in the country of bond issuance. High levels among these indicators signify good conditions for the issue of fixed-income securities by evidencing the existence of appropriate financial infrastructure. Finally, the value of government fiscal claims on the private sector variable is an indicator of the extent of state control of the private sector; the higher this figure, the greater the spread on bonds, as investors seek compensation for the risk of having to make excessive payments to the government in the form of fees, taxes, and so on.

Bond issue and issuer characteristics such as principal amount, maturity, and duration are among the key variables in the bond coupon valuation analysis and are therefore incorporated in this research as explanatory factors of bond spreads. Longer periods to maturity will expose potential investors to a greater period of risk, and will result in a higher evaluation of the risk of bond default. It should therefore be expected that higher maturity would be associated with higher spreads on bonds. The investment of large principal amounts is normally affordable only to established and prominent firms, to whom the risk of default may be negligible compared to that of small firms. It should therefore be expected that high principal amounts would have a negative effect on the bond spread. Cross-default provision (that is., the provision that if a company defaults on one of its debt obligations it will automatically default on all of its obligations) makes the risk of default higher and hence has an increasing effect on the spread. The presence of collateral on the bond, a high issuer Moody rating, and a better issuer profile (debt performance history) should be expected to have a reducing effect on the spread, as these factors serve as supporting evidence of the borrower's creditworthiness.

Firm-intrinsic characteristics should be expected also to play an important role in the default risk valuation of a bond. This paper seeks to incorporate the effects of these characteristics by including institutional and industry sector dummies characterizing the bond issuer. Securities issued by public sector entities are usually considered to be safe investments due to the government's obligation to backup debt repayments in the event of the default of the issuer company. Default risk assessment should also be expected to differ according to industry sector. The degree of state regulatory oversight imposed on the power, oil, gas, and telecommunications sectors examined in this paper differs, for example. The power sector is heavily reliant on domestic consumers and price regulations, but the export-oriented oil and gas sectors are less vulnerable to domestic regulatory shocks. Overall, it is hoped that the inclusion here of institutional and industry sector dummies will absorb the variations caused by the firm-intrinsic characteristics of the bond issuer and will therefore render unbiased the coefficients of other variables of interest.

Vagueness and instability of legislative and regulatory systems can delay projects and push costs above budget (Razavi, 1996). In order to test the impact of governance on the perception of infrastructure investment risk, this research compiled a listing of the **governance risks** attributable to a country's political, regulatory, and legal frameworks. These risks include the absence of (1) sustainable economic policy, (2) the legal and regulatory frameworks that would prevent corruption and ensure a high quality of bureaucracy, (3) contract enforcement mechanisms, (4) democratic political leadership, and (5) a system of checks and balances on political discretion; and the presence of (6) external and internal war risks and (7) risks of political expropriation and terrorism. It is expected that high levels of governance risk, encompassing an absence of democracy and lack of a stable legal framework; high political risk of confiscation, expropriation, and corruption; poor contract enforceability; and poor bureaucracy and unstable sector regulations would have a strong effect on the risk premium of a bond at its issuance and throughout its secondary market life.

4. Data

Each of the three methodological approaches of this research (cross-sectional, time-series, and downgrade history analysis) is centered on a different dependent variable. In cross-sectional analysis, this variable is the initial offer spread on fixed-rate infrastructure[8] bonds issued in U.S. dollars during 1990–99, as reported in the Euromoney Bondware database, which maintains information on all security issues in eurobonds, foreign bonds, warrants, international equities, and other capital markets. Selected according to this principle, 645 bonds were issued in 40 industrialized, emerging, and underdeveloped countries[9] by central governments (1), public corporations (48), publicly financed entities (13), public utilities (100), local governments (5), private corporations (202), privately financed entities, such as banks (177), and private utilities (98).

For the time-series analysis, this research compiled bond lifetime data on the semiannual yields of those main universe bonds that were traded in the aftermarket. The dependent variable for this approach is the annual risk premium observations on these bonds. (The annual observation was chosen to match annual changes in macro and regulatory risk factors.) The spreads were calculated by taking the difference between these yields and the yields on U.S. Treasury bonds of identical maturity, obtained by interpolating the historical U.S. government yield curve. This resulted in 26,905 weekly spread observations for 244 bonds (excluding transport bond issues) from the initial research universe of 645 infrastructure bond issues. Weekly information on yields of corporate bonds traded in the aftermarket was collected from the Bloomberg database. The spread was calculated by taking the difference between the yield to maturity of the bond and the yield to maturity of U.S. Treasury fixed income securities of the identical time to maturity.

The third methodological approach applies the events of infrastructure bond upgrades or downgrades, as assessed by independent rating agencies Standard and Poors and Moody's, over the lifetime of the bond, as registered in the Euromoney Bondware database. The dependent variable for this third approach is the triple event of the upgrade, downgrade, or no change of the bond's credit rating.

Information on independent variables was collected from a variety of sources, including the Euromoney Bondware database, which contains key fixed-income security characteristics.[10] Bond issue characteristics of an explanatory nature, as defined by this research hypothesis, were drawn from this database (see table 17).

Macroeconomic indicators characterizing the state of macroeconomic stability, commercial development, financial market development, and the extent of foreign investment were drawn from the World Bank Development Indicators database. This database contains quantitative socioeconomic information spanning five decades for all countries worldwide. The macroeconomic explanatory variables are listed in table 18.

One of the most important tasks of this research project was to collect reliable data by which to evaluate the "riskiness" of the political and regulatory environments in countries of bond issue. It is naturally difficult to measure the perception of political risk, but there are at least 14 sources worldwide, providing a variety of indexes, that attempt to assess quality of governance.[11] The World Bank describes the governance indicators in these indexes as falling into three categories: (1) objective measures describing the prevailing political and institutional arrangements—for example, the frequency of elections, organizational structure, and the size and cost of government; (2) participant surveys of interested parties, reflecting the views of citizens, entrepreneurs, foreign investors, public officials, and others on the quality of governance in their own or other countries; and (3) cross-country assessments, often entailing polls of experts who are asked to rate the quality and effectiveness of government institutions.

Much of this governance-related research is publicly available. Some risk-rating services—for example, Political Risk Services (ICRG), Standard and Poor's, and the Business Risk Service—rely on panels of experts who rate countries (or institutions within countries) using a defined set of criteria. The use of common criteria provides some comparability across countries and over time, although the ratings still depend on the experts' interpretation of the criteria and their subjective perception of each country. Other organizations—for example, the Davos World Competitiveness Report, Gallup, and the Political and Economic Risk Consultancy—rely on participant surveys. One advantage of these is that they reflect the opinions of many firms or citizens closely connected with the country they are assessing. Some surveys, however, rely on voluntary responses and ask vague questions that invite interpretation by the respondent, limiting their value for cross-country comparison.

Although the results of expert polls and participant surveys are unavoidably subjective, they often provide the best information on the less visible aspects of governance. Objective data on the prevalence of corruption are, almost by definition, difficult to obtain, leaving few alternatives to the subjective indicator. Subjective perceptions of the quality of governance are in any case often as important as simple facts. A country may have sound institutions according to objective criteria, but the confidence of its residents or investors in those institutions is also required for its governance to be assessed as good.

Analysis of the available indicators is difficult, as most of them are intercorrelated and not entirely exogenous. This paper employs cluster analysis to handle the array of regulatory and political risk indicators that are currently being produced.

For purposes of this analysis, the sources of regulatory risk indicators were selected such that they provide a measurement of the entire universe of governance risks as described in the Conceptual Framework section of this paper and, to the extent possible, that they cover all regions and years of observation presented in the selected bond universe. Following this principle, regulatory and political risk indicators were collected for the bond universe that included measurements of (1) sustainable economic policy, (2) the existence of legal and regulatory frameworks capable of preventing corruption and ensuring good bureaucracy quality, (3) contract enforceability, (4) democratic political leadership, (5) the presence of external and internal war risks, and (6) the risks of political expropriation and terrorism. These

11

data were collected from the Business Environment Risk Intelligence (BERI) Business Risk Service database, the Political Risk Service database International Country Risk Guide (ICRG), and the Transparency International Corruption Perceptions Index. The indicator for presence of a system of checks and balances on political discretion was obtained from the dissertation work of W. Henisz. Henisz developed the Political Constraints Index, which measures constraints on political opportunism and which is based solely on the number of *de jure* veto points in a given polity, maintaining the strong and unrealistic assumption of uniformly distributed preferences. This variable also accounts for the extent of the development and independence of a country's judiciary, and operates on the assumption, widely accepted in the new institutional economics literature, that the benefits of constraints on executive discretion on average outweigh the costs of lost flexibility through their ability to provide insurance against government regulatory and policy takings.

Table 1 on the following page summarizes all variables and data sources.

Table 1 Research Data and Sources

Variable	Level/type of observation	Source
Dependent		**1990–99**
Spread (difference of the yield on this bond and the yield on a U.S. Treasury bond of comparable maturity)	Fixed-rate US$ bonds issued for the power, oil, gas, telecom, and transport sectors	Euromoney Bondware
Aftermarket spread	Historical spreads for above	Bloomberg
Up(down)grade history	Binary and amount of change	Euromoney Bondware
Independent		
Country economic indicators		
Stocks traded, total value (% of GDP)	*Country*	World Bank Development Indicators Database ("SIMA")
Private nonguaranteed debt (% of ext. debt)		
Gross foreign direct investment (% of GDP)	Quantitative socioeconomic indicators	
Current revenue, excluding grants (% of GDP)		
GDP per capita, PPP (current international $)		
Inflation, consumer prices (annual %)		
Ratio of official to parallel exchange rate		
GDP growth (annual %)		
Private capital flows, total (% of GDP)		
Claims on private sector (% of GDP)		
Project characteristics		
Collaterized (yes/no)	*Bond*	Euromoney Bondware database
Callable (yes/no)		
Principal of the bond	Quantitative and descriptive bond issue characteristics	
Country of issuer		
Issuer of public sector dummy		
Issuer sector dummy (power, oil/gas, telecom, transport)		
Maturity		
Regulatory environment		
1. Economic stability; political leadership; external and internal conflict risk; corruption; military and religion in politics; law and order tradition; racial and nationality tensions; political terrorism; civil war; political party development; quality of the bureaucracy	*Country* Indexes based on expert opinion poll, 1984–98	International Country Risk Guide
2. Bureaucratic delays; contract enforceability; nationalization risk	Indexes based on expert opinion poll, 1990–95	Business Environment Risk Intelligence country index database
3. Corruption Perceptions Index	Expert survey, 1980–98	Transparency International
4. Political Constraints Index	Analysis based on de jure veto points in a country's polity, 1990–99	
5. Extent of government control; privatization progress; structure of the power sector	*Industry* Indexes based on expert survey, 1999	W. Henisz World Energy Council
6. Pricing discretion of electricity regulator	Survey of energy sector restructuring in developing countries, 1999	Energy Sector Management Assistance Program, World Bank
	International survey of electricity regulation, 1996	Cambridge University Press

5. What Drives Governance Risk Perception: Cluster Analysis of Political and Regulatory Risk Data

Cluster Segregation of the Governance Risk Indicators

The first objective of this research was the identification of those elements of government politics and regulations that dictate investor perception of political risk. Identification of the principal components of the set of 19 regulatory risk indicators compiled from the three above sources provided a convenient way to address this question. These components may be defined as the linear combinations of the original variables that are not correlated and that partition the variation in those variables in such a way that the first component carries the largest portion of the variance, and that the next component is not correlated with the first and accounts for the next-largest share of variance. The BERI, ICRG, and Transparency International data are collected from expert poll assessments of essentially the same aspects of governance. It should therefore be expected that some indicators from these databases would be highly correlated. Principal component analysis enables an exploration of the relations present in this set of data, combating possible multicollinearity problems and reducing the dimension of the data set. This form of analysis is considered highly efficient in variables clustering and variables reduction, as it clearly reveals that the variables that have similar principal component profiles essentially measure the same.

Correlation Analysis

Correlation analysis of the data set of 19 regulatory risk variables provided an initial insight into the internal relationships of the regulatory and political risk factors (see table 25). Specifically, correlation analysis identified four clusters of strong positive relationships in the set of regulatory explanatory variables.

The first cluster consists of positively correlated indicators from the ICRG database measuring the extent of (1) organized religion in politics, (2) external conflict risk, and (3) racial and nationality tensions. This relationship suggests that in a country where organized religion dominates politics, external conflict risk and racial and nationality tensions are also likely to occur. The mean correlation coefficient among variables in this cluster is 0.46, with the highest coefficient 0.62 (occurring between racial and nationality tensions and organized religion in politics) and the lowest, 0.36 (between organized religion in politics and external conflict risk).

The second cluster of highly related regulatory risk variables comprises indicators measuring the extent of (1) political party development, (2) corruption in government, (3) quality of the bureaucracy, (4) communication and transport infrastructure quality (variables from the ICRG database), (5) bureaucratic delays, (6) contract enforceability (variables from the BERI database), and (7) the Corruption Perceptions Index (Transparency International) of a given country. The mean correlation coefficient among variables in this cluster is 0.76, with the highest coefficient 0.95 (between bureaucratic delays and contract enforceability) and the lowest, 0.69 (between political party development and the Corruption Perceptions Index risks).

The third group of variables, which stands out for the vividness of intercorrelation (mean coefficient 0.75), consists of the indicators reflecting (1) the presence of the military in politics, (2) the tradition of law and order, (3) political terrorism, (4) the risk of civil war, (5) the political risk rating (variables from the ICRG database), and (6) the nationalization risk (variable from the BERI database). The highest positive relationship in this cluster is between law and order tradition and the political risk rating (0.87), with the lowest correlation occurring between the risks of political terrorism and of nationalization (0.42).

The fourth correlation cluster consists of the variables measuring (1) the effectiveness of a country's political leadership and (2) its economic policies, measured through the economic expectations versus realities and economic failures risk indicators from the ICRG database. The average correlation coefficient among the variables in this cluster is 0.76.

The close relationship between bureaucracy and corruption indicators should come as no surprise. Perhaps more thought-provoking is the link between corruption and poor bureaucracy and the broader spectrum of political risks that includes nationalization, poor contract enforceability, and the dangers of military coups, civil war, and political terrorism. This may be explained by the fact that corruption prevents democratic development (as measured by the political party development indicator) and thereby results in poor infrastructure. One of the strongest correlations across the four clusters is in fact the one between law and order tradition—an indicator that measures the historical existence of legal institutions—and democratic sustainability and the absence of corruption.

Principal Component Analysis

Principal component analysis of the regulatory risk data reinforced the findings of the initial correlation analysis. Principal Components 1 and 2 are linear combinations of regulatory risk factors, weighted as indicated (table 2). These components account for 63 and 11 percent of spread variation, respectively.

The principal components were graphically represented using the binary plot technique (see Methodology Appendix 1). When the underlying variables are highly interrelated (as is the case with the regulatory variables, which are naturally related to each other as they measure the same effect or slightly different aspects of the same effect), it often suffices to extract just the first few components to accurately describe the relationships among the underlying variables. Since the first components account for the largest portion of the variation in the

Table 2 Composition of the Two Principal Components of the Regulatory Spread Data

Regulatory risk factor	Component 1 weightings	Component 2 weightings
Economic expectations vs. realities	0.171	0.505
Economic planning failures	0.158	0.532
Politics	0.157	0.507
External conflict risk	0.103	0.048
Corruption in government	0.263	−0.157
Military in politics	0.241	−0.074
Organized religion in politics	0.187	−0.146
Law and order tradition	0.267	−0.067
Racial and nationality tensions	0.124	0.111
Political terrorism	0.212	0.087
Civil war risk	0.214	−0.034
Political party development	0.246	−0.157
Quality of the bureaucracy	0.261	−0.177
Political risk rating	0.294	0.075
Bureaucratic delays	0.283	−0.090
Contract enforceability	0.283	−0.081
Nationalization risk	0.249	0.049
Communication and transport infrastructure quality	0.265	−0.108
Corruption Perceptions Index (Transparency Int'l)	0.250	−0.191
Attributed Variance	63%	11%

Source: Author's calculations.

data, there is little left for the last components, which can therefore be dropped from the analysis without any loss of information. The accuracy of this representation is measured by the percentage of variation in the original data exhibited by the first principal components (63 and 11 percent in this case, as displayed in table 3). When the first two components are sufficient for adequate representation of the data, the principal coordinates of both observations and variables can be naturally used to construct a two-dimensional scatter plot of interrelationships between two groups of independent variables (in this instance, countries and their levels of regulatory risk) according to their values at each observation point (in this case, bond). This is known as a binary plot.

The binary plot employed here uses only the first two components extracted from the data matrix of countries and regulatory risk indicators. Each country is thus described by two coordinates (x_c, y_c), obtained by plugging the values of the regulatory variables for the country into the equations for the first and second principal components. Each regulatory risk indicator additionally receives two coordinates (x_r, y_r) given by its coefficients on these two principal component linear combinations. The binary plot technique essentially means plotting variables (various regulatory risk indicators) according to their coordinates (x_r, y_r) and observations (countries of bond issue; x_c, y_c) on the same scatter plot.

The intermediate step of binary plot construction is depicted in figure 1. Specifically, regulatory risks are positioned on the bipolar graph in accordance with their two principal component coordinates (x_r, y_r).

Figure 1 Position of Regulatory Risks in Respect to Two Principal Components

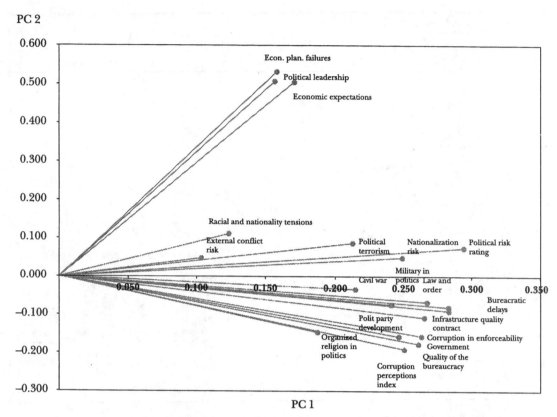

Note: X-axis – regulatory risks principal component 1 values, Y-axis – regulatory risks principal component 2 values.
Source: Author's calculations.

The advantage of the binary plot technique is that it allows the researcher to examine the clusters of variables and observations within the underlying multidimensional space. The cosines between the vectors-variables reflect the underlying correlations; the projections of the observations onto these vectors are proportional to their standardized values.

The four clusters of regulatory risk indicators visible in figure 1 signify that regulatory risks within the clusters possess similar (close) coefficients on two principal components and are closely related. As can be seen from the graph, three out of four clusters of independent regulatory variables have close coefficients.

For the binary plot on figure 2, the regulatory risk indicator variables were centered and standardized for each country (that is, the mean was removed from each value and the result divided by the standard deviation) prior to extracting the principal components, thereby resulting in all vectors being of the same unit length. Note that if two variables were closely correlated, their corresponding vectors on the binary plot would be almost collinear. Similarly, if two countries shared similar values for all regulatory variables, they would also be situated closely on the binary plot.

Figure 2 Bond Country of Issuance Position on Regulatory Risk Indicator Vectors

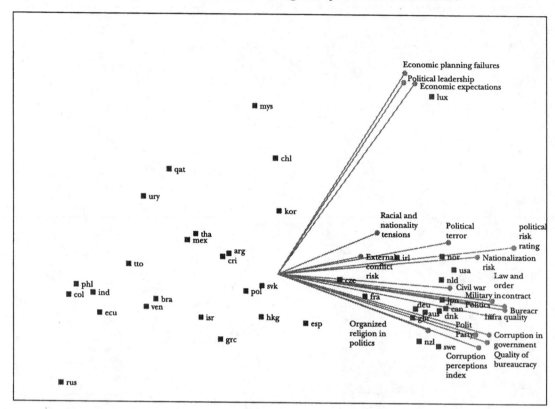

Note: X-axis – regulatory risks principal component 1 values, Y-axis – regulatory risks principal component 2 values.
Source: Author's calculations.

A visual inspection of figure 2 reveals that regulatory risk indicators form four distinct groups, three of which are quite closely related. These groups essentially replicate the groups identified through earlier correlation and principal component analysis. On this biplot, the intersection of the rays indicates the mean values for all variables, with each of the rays on the plot representing the positive half-axes of the underlying variable. The viewer can approximately reconstruct the regulatory riskiness of any one country, as measured by any of the individual risk indicators, by making a perpendicular projection from that country onto the line that contains the corresponding ray. (As depicted, the rays indicate the positive semi-axes of the variables. The negative extensions of these rays, although not drawn on the graph, may be easily made to accommodate the projection.) For example, by making projections to the ray of the appropriate governance risk, in may be established that Korea has high economic planning and political leadership ratings, but a relatively poor rating for external conflict risk. The United States, Canada, and Norway have excellent (high) ratings for immunity against virtually all political and regulatory risks, as their projections fall farthest away from the origin in the positive direction.

Hierarchical Cluster Analysis of Regulatory Risk Data

Principal component analysis of the regulatory risk data and earlier correlation calculations may be further supplemented by hierarchical cluster analysis of the regulatory risk indicators data. The idea behind cluster analysis is to combine universe observations into groups (clusters) based on some criteria of similarity. The techniques of cluster analysis differ according to the way that these similarities are computed and accounted for when building the clusters. With hierarchical methods, the partition of observations into clusters is achieved sequentially. Each observation is initially considered a separate cluster, with the closest clusters then merged into bigger groups. This process can be graphically represented as a dendrogram (see Annex G). The distance between two clusters is defined by Ward's formula, which measures the increase in intra-class distances after the two clusters are merged. Minimization of this distance maximizes the reduction of inter-cluster variation, which is a goal of cluster analysis.

Hierarchical cluster analysis yielded the following groupings of regulatory risk indicators (table 3). These groupings are fully consistent with the results of the correlation, principal component, and binary plot analyses:

Challenges Posed by Subjective Governance Indicators

A common concern about governance indicators, both political and regulatory, is that they can be inconsistent, unreliable, or affected by bias on the part of the observer. A country rated high by one agency or panel of experts may be rated low by another, even though both claim

Table 3 Clusters of Governance Risk Factors

Fundamentalism risks	*Economic policy sustainability risks*	*Corruption and autocracy risks*	*Political disorder risks*
Organized religion in politics	Political leadership	Political party development	Law and order tradition
External conflict risk	Economic planning failures	Corruption in government	Civil war risks
Racial and nationality tensions	Economic expectations vs. realities	Quality of the bureaucracy	Military in politics
		Infrastructure quality	Political terrorism
		Corruption	Political risk rating
		Perceptions Index	Nationalization risk
		Bureaucratic delays	
		Contract enforceability	

Source: Author's calculations.

to measure the same attribute. Recent research by Kaufmann, Kraay, and Zoido-Lobatón (1999) proposed that this problem might be resolved by aggregating indicators from several sources into an average or composite index—a poll of polls. This is the approach that Transparency International uses for its Perceptions of Corruption Index. The researchers found that individual governance indicators may be imprecise, but that an aggregation of indicators from many different sources can improve the precision of cross-country comparisons of governance. Aggregate indicators are not so precise that small differences between country scores can be given much significance, but they do enable clear identification of the best and worst performers with a reasonable degree of statistical confidence. As a general rule, the more sources used, the greater the precision of the assessments made.

Most of the analysis made in this paper is based on aggregate estimates of regulatory risk factors. Specifically, two principal components and the averages across identified clusters were used to explain spread variation. The influence of individual risk ratings was also tested, yielding valuable information on the impact of each on the spread. These tests show that the aggregate indexes across these four groups have greater explanatory power than most of the individual indexes.

Correlation of the Spread and Regulatory Cluster Averages

Further correlation analysis of the relationship between the spread and the regulatory risk data showed that the regulatory risk characteristics within four identified regulatory risk clusters affect the spread differently. By taking the means of all indicators within a given risk cluster and correlating them with the log of spread, it was determined that the mean of indicators within the corruption and autocracy risk cluster (comprising political party development, corruption in government, the quality of the bureaucracy, communication infrastructure quality and measurements, bureaucratic delays, and contract enforceability) account for most of the bond spread variation (correlation coefficient –0.67, with significance at 99 percent level).[12] The mean of indicators within the political disorder risks cluster (civil war risks, the military in politics, law and order tradition, political terrorism, and nationalization risk) is also highly correlated with the spread, with a coefficient of –0.504, significant at the 99 percent level. The regulatory risk variables from the two other risk clusters were found to have a weaker relationship or no relationship with the spread: the average of regulatory risk indicators from the fundamentalism risk cluster has no significant relationship with the spread, and the average of the sound economic policy sustainability risk indicator has a weak negative relationship within the spread, having a correlation coefficient of –0.182, significant at 99 percent level. Interestingly, the average of BERI characteristics (bureaucratic delays, contract enforceability, and nationalization risk) appears to have the highest significant coefficient for correlation with the log of spread, of –0.715 at 99 percent level. This may be explained by the weighted presence of representative characteristics from the corruption and autocracy risks cluster and the political disorder risks cluster in this grouping of regulatory risk indicators (table 4).

This analysis shows that there are governance-related risks that investors can avoid and risks that they cannot. Specifically, investors can diversify away some political and economic

Table 4 Correlation Coefficients of Main Regulatory Risk Indicator Clusters and the Log of Spread

	Log spread	*Funda-mentalism risk cluster*	*Corruption/ autocracy risk cluster*	*Economic policy risk cluster*	*Political disorder risk cluster*	*BERI average*	*Political constraints*
Log spread	1.000						
Fundamentalism risks average	0.012	1.000					
Corruption and autocracy average	−0.670***	0.061	1.000				
Economic policy sustainability average	−0.182***	−0.075**	0.228***	1.000			
Political disorder risks average	−0.504***	0.300***	0.735***	0.306***	1.000		
BERI average	−0.715***	0.099***	0.942***	0.255***	0.690***	1.000	
Political Constraints Index	−0.371***	−0.007	0.547***	0.062	0.406***	0.479***	1.000

Notes: *** – denotes significance at 1 percent level; ** – denotes significance at 5 percent level.
Source: Author's calculations.

leadership incompetence and some erratic economic policies. However, they cannot diversify away the effects of systemic incentives to steal (corruption) or to break commitments (poor contract enforceability), which together reduce expected values and make necessary an offsetting spread. These preliminary findings are examined in greater detail in the later stages of this study through regression analysis of bond credit structure.

Country Clustering by the Level of Political Risk

Another notable result of the principal component analysis is the clear segregation of countries into three regulatory/political risk groups. Under binary plotting, if two variables are closely correlated their corresponding vectors on the biplot will be almost collinear. Likewise, if two countries have similar values for all regulatory variables, they will be situated closely on the biplot. Segregation of countries into clusters is done by measuring their distance from the average level of risk on all regulatory risk indicators; here, the intersection point of the regulatory risk vector rays. According to the theoretical foundation of the biplot, countries that are situated far on the positive side of the Y and X axes possess excellent governance characteristics and may be considered virtually free of political and regulatory problems. These countries may be termed stable. Countries that are situated around the beginning of the axis possess average levels in their regulatory risk indicators, and may be termed "weak." Finally, countries that lie far on the negative side of the Y and X axes are relevant outliers with high levels of political and regulatory risk, and are termed risky.

Table 5 Country Classification by Regulatory Riskiness

Stable	*Weak*	*Risky*
Austria	Argentina	Brazil
Canada	Chile	Colombia
Denmark	Costa Rica	Dominican Republic
France	Czech Republic	Ecuador
Germany	Greece	India
Ireland	Hong Kong	Israel
Japan	Korea, Republic of	Philippines
Luxembourg	Malaysia	Russia
Netherlands	Mexico	Trinidad and Tobago
New Zealand	Poland	Uruguay
Norway	Qatar	Venezuela
Sweden	Slovak Republic	
United Kingdom	Spain	
United States	Thailand	

Source: Author's classification.

The visual evidence provided by the biplot is supported by hierarchical cluster analysis of the country regulatory risk data. Cluster analysis yielded the following groupings of countries, classified according to their regulatory riskiness (table 5).

Figure 3 Regulatory Riskiness of Bond Issuer Countries

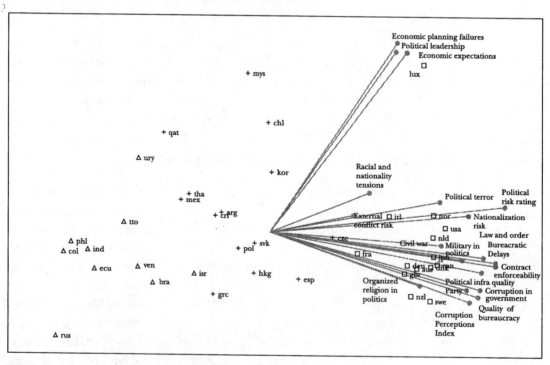

Note: Symbols: □ countries from Stable category ; + – Weak category; Δ – Risky category.
X-axis – principal component 1 values, Y-axis – principal component 2 values
Source: Author's calculations.

The following binary plot chart illustrates this finding using three different symbols to denote the group distribution of country observation points (figure 3).

This segregation of the countries of the research universe according to risk perception is supported by measurement of the average spread on infrastructure bonds. The total spread average across all years of the countries identified here as stable is 136.57; for the weak countries it is 231.72; and for the risky countries it is 305.34. Further, the standard deviation by year from the average spread for the entire universe of countries is in most cases higher than that for each of the three country groups (table 6).[13]

These results suggest that there is a clear separation of countries into three regulatory and political risk clusters. The least developed countries and countries struggling in transition generally have poor governance indicators and have to pay high premiums to encourage investment. Governance issues are similarly a major challenge for the emerging economies, which must act to defuse a wide range of political and regulatory risks. The developed countries alone are in the clear. The reasons for and the nature of the three regulatory quality clusters—and their policy implications—are analyzed in greater detail later in this paper.

Table 6 Spread Behavior in Three Regulatory Risk Country Groups

Year	Spread data	Evaluation of regulatory environment (based on biplot analysis)			
		Stable	Weak	Risky	Total
1991	Average	55.43	282.50	465.75	216.62
	Standard deviation	22.44	53.03	133.76	203.78
1992	Average	51.67	259.67	421.33	234.20
	Standard deviation	17.23	96.93	138.54	189.24
1993	Average	63.30	248.91	289.25	170.90
	Standard deviation	35.01	141.20	100.85	139.42
1994	Average	60.83	310.71	335.38	189.96
	Standard deviation	52.09	139.85	89.85	160.42
1995	Average	121.00	197.33	335.83	174.88
	Standard deviation	165.59	175.86	65.99	172.54
1996	Average	90.77	200.55	244.22	172.99
	Standard deviation	169.09	149.56	107.76	159.40
1997	Average	141.41	182.29	259.97	184.09
	Standard deviation	172.85	114.62	155.16	153.36
1998	Average	227.27	280.53	300.44	249.24
	Standard deviation	223.29	168.77	186.85	205.88
Total universe average		136.57	231.72	305.34	199.05
Number of countries		212	159	83	459
Standard deviation		177.45	150.78	139.76	174.16

Source: Author's calculations.

6. Impact of Governance Risks on Investment Cost at Entry: Analysis of Cross-Sectional At-Issuance Spread Data

Impact of Country (Macro)-Level Regulatory Risks

Data Layout and Basic Model

This paper uses an augmented multifactor logistic risk spread model to analyze the determinants of the yield spread on bonds. Similar models have been used by Edwards (1986), Angbazo and others (1996), and Eichengreen and Mody (1997) to study different aspects of the formation processes of bond and loan spreads. For the purposes of this study, yield spreads on bonds are determined as follows:

Model 1

$$log\ (S_{it}) = F(X_{it}) + e_{it}$$

The dependent variable is defined as the logarithm of the spread S_{it} over a benchmark (U.S. Treasury) of bonds issued to finance infrastructure projects in country i in year t. X_{it} is the vector of independent variables, which will be used to measure how the credit risk premium is related to a set of explanatory variables. Log of spread is a traditional measure of the risk premium that bond issuers have to pay investors to undertake the risk of a principal and interest loss. (Detailed specifications of the model may be found in Methodology Appendix 2.)

Model 1 accounts for the effects of the three types of risk variables—macroeconomic, political-regulatory, and firm or project-intrinsic—that according to research hypotheses affect the spread. Based on the analyses outlined in Section 3, the variables in table 7 were selected to test the research hypotheses through model A OLS regression fitting.

The dummy identifying the sector—public or private—of the issuer was constructed as follows: (1) public issuer type to encompass public utility, public corporate, central government, and public finance (total 162 bonds); (2) private issuer type to encompass private utility, private corporate, private finance, and supranational (total 482 bonds). Three dummies

24

were additionally constructed to identify the sector of bond issuer: power, telecom, and oil and gas.

More on Choice of Independent Variables

To prevent the problem of multicollinearity, variables that were insignificant in their relationship with the spread or highly correlated among each other (or both) were manually discarded following the principle of R square maximization and significance level threshold. Among the macroeconomic characteristics, two variables were discarded as endogenous and highly correlated with GDP per capita: these were claims on the private sector (correlation coefficient 0.66) and current revenue (0.40). (Table 19 indicates correlations among the macro variables.) The indicator measuring the level of private nonguaranteed debt was also discarded as being insignificant in explaining the spread.

Among the bond issue characteristics, two variables (cross default and collateral provisions) were discarded from the regression analysis as being not significantly related to the dependent variable. The Moody's issuer rating was additionally excluded for the reason that it is an expert index—that is, a variable constructed based on evaluation of fundamental country and bond issue characteristics, both of which are already included in this regression. It is important to note that the regression of the log of spread on three variables—GDP per capita, the Moody's issuer rating, and the regulatory risk rating (average BERI)—resulted in significant coefficients on all of these variables, however. This observation suggests that the rating agency (in this case, Moody's) does not take into account the entire regulatory risk associated with the country and sector of bond issuance.

Of the regulatory variables, the following were used in the OLS regression tests: (1) the two principal components identified in section 5.1; (2) the averages for indicators within four governance risk clusters (that is, the corruption and autocracy risk cluster, the political disorder risk cluster, the fundamentalism risk cluster, and the economic policy sustainability risk

Table 7 Variables Selection for Step 2 OLS Regression Analysis of the Spread

Macroeconomic	*Political/regulatory*	*Financial/bond*
Real GDP per capita	Average values for 4 governance risk clusters (Fundamentalism,	Principal amount of the bond
Gross foreign direct investment as percentage of GDP	Economic Policy, Corruption and Autocracy, and Political Disorder)	Public sector type of bond issuer (dummy)
Volume of stocks traded as percentage of GDP	BERI Average (bureaucratic delays, contract enforceability, nationalization risk	Industry sector of bond issuer (dummy)
GDP growth	Two principal components	
	Political constraints index	

Source: Author's selection.

clusters); (3) the average of three BERI indexes; and (4) the Political Constraints Index measuring the number of veto points in a given polity.

Table 8 summarizes the results of the regression on macro-level regulatory risks. (Results for industry-level regulatory risks specific to the power sector are provided in a separate chapter.) Table 8 presents the results of the ordinary least squares regression of the infrastructure bond spreads and the financial, macroeconomic, political, and regulatory risk characteristics. Each of the equations includes independent variables measuring (1) real GDP per capita, adjusted for inflation; (2) the country's volume of stocks traded, as a percentage of GDP; (3) gross foreign direct investment as a percentage of GDP; (4) GDP growth rate; (5) the principal amount of the bond; (6) a dummy indicating if the issuer is a public or private sector institution; (7) dummies indicating if the bond was issued for the power, oil and gas, telecommunications, or transport sector; and (8) a variable reflecting the extent of governance risk in the country, measured by the average corruption and autocracy cluster regulatory risk rating, the average of BERI ratings, the average of the political disorder risk rating, the Political Constraints Index, and, in one instance, by two principal components of regulatory risk data.

Results for the Entire Sample Universe

The first three columns of table 8 present experiments to explain the spread structure through different combinations of governance risk indicators. The equation in column 1 shows the effect of using these control variables to explain the relative spreads for the sample universe of infrastructure bonds. The first model is tested with uses the two principal components of regulatory risk data and the Political Constraints Index to account for the impact of regulatory risks on bond spreads. The results indicate with a likelihood of not less than 99 percent that spreads would rise by 22.2, 21.2 and 20.5 basis points were bonds to be issued in the power, oil and gas, and telecommunications sectors, respectively. These dummy variables essentially absorb the effect of firm-intrinsic risks on the risk premium. There is a 99 percent probability that the spreads would be lower by 14.2 basis points if the principal of the bond were one year longer. Unit increases in the volume of stocks traded annually, as a percentage of GDP, and in real GDP per capita decrease the bond spread by 21.4 and 26.3 basis points respectively, with a confidence level of 1 percent. Higher levels of FDI increase the risk perception of the bond by 8.9 points with 90 percent probability. This contradicts the intuitive assumption that this variable is a sign of a country's stability. Public sector ownership of a project reduces investor perceptions of a bond's default risk, reducing the spread by 22.2 basis points with 99 percent probability. This finding conforms to the general Wall Street convention that private sector bonds cannot be priced below the sovereign ceiling. Finally, the two principal components of regulatory risk data and higher regulatory risk ratings (indicating safer governance conditions in the country of bond issue) decrease the risk premium by 38 and 11.6 basis points respectively, with a confidence level of 1 percent. This set of control variables can explain about 63.4 percent of the spread variance.

The equation in column 2 comprises a slightly different list of explanatory variables. Specifically, the two principal components of regulatory and political risk data are replaced

Table 8 Results of Log Spread Regression on Selected Independent Variables

Variable name	Sample										
	Entire w/ 2 reg. PCs	Entire w/ 2 reg. clusters	Entire w/ BERI	Stable countries	Weak countries	Risky countries	Public issuers	Private issuers	Power sector	Oil/gas sector	Telecom sector
Principal	-.142*** (.001)	-.139*** (.001)	-.126*** (.001)	-.118 (.170)	-.198*** (.000)	-.239** (.022)	-.127** (.003)	-.075 (.338)	-.165** (.034)	-.229*** (.000)	-.046 (.664)
Real GDP per capita	-.263*** (.000)	-.270*** (.000)	-.217*** (.000)	-.099 (.198)	-.108** (.033)	-.463*** (.003)	-.221*** (.001)	-.209* (.094)	-.114 (.241)	-.143 (.151)	-.513*** (.001)
GDP growth	.019 (.605)	-.014 (.698)	-.007 (.846)	.007 (.928)	.035 (.392)	-.012 (.907)	.018 (.608)	-.012 (.873)	-.082 (.155)	.036 (.579)	.016 (.835)
Stock volume	-.214*** (.000)	-.227*** (.000)	-.164*** (.001)	.262** (.016)	-.413*** (.000)	-.281** (.008)	-.207*** (.000)	-.073 (.607)	-.166** (.016)	-.159** (.050)	-.230** (.043)
Public sector	-.222*** (.000)	-.221*** (.000)	-.214*** (.000)	-.485*** (.000)	-.028 (.546)	-.054 (.674)	n.a.	n.a.	-.118* (.061)	-.220*** (.001)	-.356*** (.000)
Power sector	.212*** (.000)	.200*** (.001)	.198*** (.001)	.616*** (.000)	-.019 (.848)	.345** (.047)	.054 (.571)	.202** (.018)	n.a.	n.a.	n.a.
Oil and gas	.205*** (.000)	.174** (.002)	.163** (.003)	.354*** (.001)	-.094 (.351)	.296** (.047)	.001 (.994)	.279** (.002)	n.a.	n.a.	n.a.
Telecom	.200*** (.000)	.182*** (.001)	.190*** (.000)	.393*** (.001)	-.019 (.848)	.327** (.040)	-.019 (.818)	.374*** (.000)	n.a.	n.a.	n.a.
Foreign direct investment	.089* (.072)	.105** (.029)	.014 (.769)	.304** (.034)	.053 (.504)	.143 (.361)	-.052 (.255)	.182* (.058)	-.053 (.399)	-.219** (.049)	.284* (.024)
BERI average	n.a.	n.a.	-.474*** (.000)	.285 (.121)	-.550*** (.000)	-.312** (.007)	-.492** (.008)	-.512*** (.000)	-.513*** (.00)	-.471*** (.000)	-.327** (.016)
Regulatory PC1	-.380*** (.000)	n.a.	n.a.	n.a.	n.a.	n.a.	n.a.	n.a.	n.a.	n.a.	n.a.
Regulatory PC2	-.116** (.004)	n.a.	n.a.	n.a.	n.a.	n.a.	n.a.	n.a.	n.a.	n.a.	n.a.
Political disorder	n.a.	.000 (.997)	n.a.	n.a.	n.a.	n.a.	n.a.	n.a.	n.a.	n.a.	n.a.
Autocracy and corruption	n.a.	-.422 (.000)	n.a.	n.a.	n.a.	n.a.	n.a.	n.a.	n.a.	n.a.	n.a.
Political constraints index	-.049 (.152)	.009 (.857)	n.a.	-.155 (.022)	n.a.	n.a.	n.a.	n.a.	n.a.	n.a.	n.a.
Degree of freedom	304	304	304	130	107	65	196	107	109	88	63
R square	.634	.645	.661	.378	.864	.561	.787	.526	.701	.742	.693

Note: Dependent variable – log of bond spread.
n.a. Not available.
*** – Denotes significance at 1 percent level; ** – denotes significance at 5 percent level; * – denotes significance at 10 level. Figures in parentheses are two tail p-values.
Source: Author's calculations.

by the averages of the two regulatory risk clusters that were identified as having the highest significant correlation with the spread—that is, the autocracy and corruption and the political disorder risk clusters. This change increases the explanatory power of the model, bringing it to 64.5 percent of the variance. An increase of one unit in the country's average autocracy and corruption risk indicators is predicted to decrease the spread by about 42.2 basis points. When measured through regression analysis, the political disorder risks are found to have no significant relationship with the spread—this lack of significance may be explained by the high correlation between the variables within the red tape and political disorder clusters. Other coefficients drawn from the remaining independent variables have the same signs and relatively the same magnitude as in column 1.

Column 3 presents the results generated by a model including the governance risk indicator as measured by the average of three BERI ratings (contract enforceability, bureaucratic delays, and nationalization risk).[14] This group of risks was chosen for this and subsequent expression of the spread due to its strongest relationship with the spread, as defined by the earlier correlation analysis. Indeed, inclusion of this variable in the regression analysis improves considerably the explanatory capacity of the model, as measured by an R square of 0.661. According to the estimation results for this model, an improvement in the average BERI rating in a country results in a decrease of the spread by 47.4 basis points. Coefficients drawn from the other independent variables have the same signs and relatively the same magnitude as in columns 1 and 2.

Results of Three Country Groups

The equations in columns 4 through 6 test whether or not the effect of the above factors on the spread is consistent when the universe of countries is subdivided into three groups according to their level of regulatory risk, as defined earlier (see table below).

Countries Classification by Level of Governance Risk

Stable	Weak	Risky
Austria	Argentina	Brazil
Canada	Chile	Colombia
Denmark	Costa Rica	Dominican Republic
France	Czech Republic	Ecuador
Germany	Greece	India
Ireland	Hong Kong	Israel
Japan	Korea, Republic of	Philippines
Luxembourg	Malaysia	Russia
Netherlands	Mexico	Trinidad and Tobago
New Zealand	Poland	Uruguay
Norway	Qatar	Venezuela
Sweden	Slovak Republic	
UK	Spain	
USA	Thailand	

Source: Author's calculations.

Stable Countries (Good Governance)

For the group of stable countries (column 4), the explanatory power of the model was significantly lower than for the entire universe of bonds, explaining only about 37.8 percent of the dependent variable variation. This finding suggests that the model does not have sufficient elements to perfectly replicate the conditions of bond pricing decisions in politically and regulatorily stable countries. As suggested by earlier literature, the explanatory power of the regression could be improved by adding more firm-financial, industry, and capital-market status characteristics to the right hand side of the equation.

The results shown in column 4 indicate that political risk, as might be expected, has no influence on the bond risk pricing decision in regulatory risk-free countries. The same is true of the GDP growth variable, and there is only a weak positive relationship between the spread and volume of stocks traded and FDI levels in these countries. The only macroeconomic variable that has a significant negative relationship on the spread is real GDP per capita, with a unit increase in real GDP per capita shown as likely to decrease the spread by 41.0 basis points. Richer countries have it cheaper. With the general weakness of other macroeconomic and governance factors, it is the financial and industry sector characteristics of bond issues that stand out as having a substantial effect on the spreads in these countries: the spread increases by 61.6 basis points if a bond is issued in the power sector and by 35.4 and 39.3 basis points if it is issued in the oil and gas and telecommunications sectors, respectively. The high coefficient on the power sector dummy is not casual—the power sector in developed countries is often subject to heavy price, quality, and environmental regulation, which can bring financial losses to the company and hence increases the probability of default. In addition, in some countries of this group the deregulation process adds to the uncertainties associated with bond payments. Bond issuance by a public sector entity reduces the risk spread by 51.5 basis points.

Essentially, these results certify that in countries in the stable group, infrastructure investments are free of political and regulatory uncertainty and the only factors affecting the lender's decision are the financials of the project (represented by the yield to maturity) and the industry factor (captured by one of the industry sector dummies). Another important observation is that in stable countries, it is energy/utility investments that bear the highest level of risk.

Countries with Weak Governance

Column 5 presents OLS regression evidence on the association between the above set of variables and the spreads on bonds from the second group of countries—those characterized by weak governance. Here the R square is significantly higher than that for the entire universe and for the group of stable countries (approximately 86.4 percent of the spread variance), suggesting that the research model is best suited for estimation of bond pricing decisions for regulatorily weak countries. The results of this regression are thought provoking. The significant coefficients have the expected signs and include only the political/regulatory risk rating (BERI), financial (principal amount of the loan), and macroeconomic (GDP per capita and volume of stocks traded) factors. Political risk carries most of the weight (a unit increase in average BERI rating decreases the spread by 55 basis points with 99 percent probability), followed by the volume of stocks traded as a percentage of GDP and real GDP per capita. A 1 percent increase in stocks volume decreases the spread on bonds by 41.3 basis points with 99 percent probability. Larger principal bond issues are also viewed as less risky, with 95 percent confidence. It is also noteworthy that public sector association of the bond issuer has no significant positive effect on the bond credit risk spread, unlike in the stable country group—suggesting that a guarantee made by a weak state is not considered a protection. Finally, sector dummies measuring industry and firm-intrinsic characteristics have no explanatory power. The latter suggests that firm-intrinsic characteristics are less relevant to fixed-income securities pricing in emerging markets. Poor governance affects even the most-efficient businesses.

Countries with Poor Governance

Results for the risky countries are summarized in column 6. The explanatory power of this regression is smaller than that for weak countries, explaining about 56.1 percent of the spread variation. Bond pricing in these countries reflects their macroeconomic (real GDP per capita, volume of stocks traded, GDP growth), bond (principal amount), sector (power sector dummy), and regulatory risk (average BERI) characteristics. The coefficient on the regulatory risk variable is less precise and has a smaller effect on the spread, decreasing it by 31.2 basis points with 95 percent confidence. Macroeconomic characteristics, including real GDP per capita and the volume of stocks traded, and the principal amount of the bond are all negatively related with the spread and are significant at the 5 percent level. Industry and firm-intrinsic risk factors are positively related to the spread with 95 percent likelihood, increasing it by 34.5, 29.6, and 32.7 basis points for the power, oil and gas, and telecommunications sectors, respectively.

To summarize, regression analysis of the spread within the three country clusters reveals that the types of risks that concern investors differ across these clusters. The least developed countries and countries struggling with transition generally have very poor governance indicators and have to offer high premiums to encourage investment. Emerging economies, which may already have in place appropriate fiscal and other macroeconomic policies and ownership structures, also face governance issues as their toughest challenge, as they seek to remove a whole range of political and regulatory risks. Developed countries alone are in the clear, with investors concerned only about real commercial project risk rather than about policy risk created by adverse actions of governments.

Public Sector Entity Bonds

The next step of the regression analysis assessed differences in the risk pricing of private and public sector infrastructure bonds. Columns 7 and 8 present the results of this assessment. For public sector projects, the model yielded a high explanatory power, as measured by R square of 0.787. Here, the firm- and sector-intrinsic characteristics measured by sector dummies have no influence over the risk spread, a fact that can be attributed to state backing of public sector infrastructure projects. The factors of greatest significance in the risk assessment of public sector bond issues are real GDP per capita, the volume of stocks traded, the principal amount, and the regulatory risk rating. The latter has the greatest coefficient and decreases the spread with one unit of rating increase by 49.2 basis points at the 1 percent confidence level. Political climate and a country's macroeconomic characteristics are of the greatest importance for investors in public sector-sponsored infrastructure projects.

Private Sector Entity Bonds

For private sector projects, the regression estimation model yielded results of a smaller explanatory power (R square 0.526). This might indicate that the model is less suited for explanation of privately issued bond spreads than it is for publicly issued ones, and it is likely that a model taking greater account of firm-intrinsic and capital market performance variables would provide a better explanation of the spreads of such bonds. In contrast to the case of public sector infrastructure investments, what matters most here are the political and regulatory risk factors and the firm- and sector-intrinsic characteristics of bond issue. A unit increase in the regulatory risk rating decreases the risk spread by 51.2 basis points at the 1 percent confidence level. Macroeconomic characteristics, except for (weakly) real GDP per capita and the level of foreign direct investment, do not play a major role in the pricing decision for these bonds as companies are expected to evaluate the macroeconomic climate and be able to compensate for that climate with the economic efficiency of their projects. Regulatory risk, in contrast, appears to be a crucial factor, and one that can impede the ability of private sector infrastructure firms to adjust to macroeconomic conditions. Firm- and industry-intrinsic characteristics also play an important role in determining the risk premium structure of private sector infrastructure bonds.

Sector Differences

Columns 9 through 11 present the results of an estimating spread model for the four infrastructure sectors represented in the bond research universe. For column 9, the model is estimated on a subset of power sector bonds to identify the determinants of the lender's risk premium pricing decision in the case of power sector projects. The regression yields a relatively high R square, explaining about 70.1 percent of the dependent variable's variation. The coefficients on independent variables are significant and have the expected signs for volume of stocks traded and public sector dummy. The coefficient on political risk indicator (average BERI) is positive, is of high magnitude, and is highly significant, which suggests that a unit increase in the regulatory risk rating would reduce the spread by 51.3 basis points.

The determinants for oil and gas and telecommunications bonds are explored in a similar fashion in columns 10 and 11. The explanatory power of these models is also fairly high, with R squares of 0.742 and 0.693, respectively. The models for these subgroups of infrastructure bonds provided results similar to those of the power sector, with real GDP per capita additionally proving significant in the telecom sector and the principal bond amount significant in oil and gas. The public sector dummy has even greater significance in decreasing the risk of bond default in these sectors than in the power sector. Another important distinction between the power and the oil and gas and telecommunications sectors is that political and regulatory risk (as indicated by the coefficient on the average BERI) is less important for oil and gas and telecom projects than for power projects. This finding supports the hypothesis that power sector investments are riskier from the political perspective, because the product is consumer-oriented and serves the entire voter base, and is therefore highly susceptible to government price control and other regulations.

The results of this regression make it possible to estimate the cost of governance-borne risks in emerging bond markets. Substitution into the spread equation of the values obtained for the independent variables gives a proxy of the costs of regulatory and political risks to infrastructure bond issuers, calculated as spread payments that could have been avoided, of about $677.7 million in 1997. [15]

Impact of Country-Level Governance Risk Factors on the Spread

An important goal of this research is to establish the impact of various political and regulatory risks on the risk price of infrastructure bonds. To estimate the "pure" impact on bond risk premiums of the individual components of the ICRG, BERI, and Transparency International index groups—as opposed to the composite indexes (BERI average and principal components) used in the above regression analyses—the spread model was separately tested with each of the regulatory and political risk indexes. Tables B.1 and B.2 at the end of this paper present the full results of these regressions. Table 9 compares the effects of each of these factors on the spread.

Table 9 Results of Spread Regression on Various Governance Risk Factors

Risk factor name	Standardized coefficient	P–value	R–square
Corruption and autocracy risks cluster average	−.414***	.000	.645
Political disorder risks cluster average	−.166**	.002	.601
Economic policy sustainability risks cluster average	.082*	.063	.592
Fundamentalism risks cluster average	−.046	.246	.589
Communication and transport infrastructure quality (BERI)	−.536***	.000	.648
Bureaucratic delays (BERI)	−.382***	.000	.631
Contract enforceability (BERI)	−.301***	.000	.614
Corruption Perceptions Index (TI)	−.269***	.000	.618
Political party development	−.265***	.000	.649
Quality of the bureaucracy	−.248***	.000	.614
Corruption in government	−.245***	.000	.620
Nationalization risk	−.240***	.000	.601
Law and order tradition	−.173***	.006	.599
External conflict risk	−.081**	.032	.595
Political terrorism	−.066	.151	.591
Racial and nationality tensions	−.048	.263	.590
Economic expectations vs. realities	.042	.340	.590
Civil war	−.047	.370	.590
Military in politics	.044	.395	.590
Political leadership	−.027	.540	.589
Organized religion in politics	−.011	.781	.589
Economic planning failures	−.009	.844	.589

Note: * – denotes significance at 10 percent level; ** – denotes significance at 5 percent level; *** – denotes significance at 1 percent level.
Source: Author's calculations.

Table 9 lists the individual political and regulatory risks in order of the magnitude of their impact. Transparent and efficient bureaucratic systems, the absence of corruption, and the presence of democracy are shown to be the most effective tools in reducing the risk perception of an investor in infrastructure bonds. These factors are followed in importance by the traditional political risks of nationalization, expropriation, and war. The regressions of the spread on individual regulatory risk indicators are fully consistent with the findings of the earlier principal component and correlation analysis.

Test for Universe Selection Bias—Truncated Regression

The bonds included in this universe were by default all subject to conditions of issuance—that is, they were all issued in an environment that the issuer deemed to be equal or above an acceptable safety threshold. No bonds have ever been issued in an environment deemed too risky. This raises the concern that the universe of bonds is biased. Information on defunct projects that were initiated and aborted, or in which the issue of bonds otherwise failed, would potentially serve to redress this bias, but consistent information on such bonds is unfortunately not available.

The econometric technique of truncated regression was used to test the potential of a selectivity bias and to obtain a more accurate (unbiased) estimate of the regression coefficients (table 10). Truncated regression relies on the assumption that information is only available on successful projects for which $Y < c$, where Y is the spread and c is a threshold that may be interpreted as the maximum spread (serving as an investment environment risk indicator) allowable for a project to be financed through a bond issue. (Detailed specifications of the truncated regression test are outlined in Methodology Appendix 3.) Should the selection bias be strong, the truncated regression would result in coefficients of significantly larger magnitude. In this case, the truncated coefficients were found to be larger but not significantly so, suggesting that the sample bias is not large and that the previous analyses are therefore legitimate.

Table 10 Coefficients of the End Result of Automated Stepwise Regression

Variable	Nonstandardized coefficients of truncated regression	Nonstandardized coefficients of OLS regression
Currency amount	−.000258 (.172)	−.000254 (.170)
Real GDP per capita	−.099*** (.000)	−.092*** (.001)
Stocks traded	−.189*** (.000)	−.178*** (.000)
GDP growth	−.007 (.643)	−.006 (.692)
BERI	−.854*** (.000)	−.846*** (.000)
Power	.607*** (.000)	.581*** (.000)
Oil/gas	.503*** (.000)	.428*** (.000)
Telecom	.711*** (.000)	.682*** (.000)
Issuer public	−.627*** (.000)	−.589*** (.000)
R square	.646	.642

Note: *** – denotes significance at 1 percent level. Figures in parentheses are p–values.
Source: Author's calculations.

Model Application: Estimation of Infrastructure Bond Spreads in the Czech Republic and Hungary

As a case study, the research applied the model developed here to estimate the expected risk return for infrastructure investors in two transition economies, the Czech Republic and Hungary, in 1997. The Czech Republic notably issued more infrastructure bonds than any other Central and Eastern European country; Hungary, in contrast, preferred other types of infrastructure financing.[16]

Infrastructure Finance in Western and Eastern Europe

European countries are increasingly using bonds to fund infrastructure development. Table 11 summarizes the information on all infrastructure bonds issued in the countries of Central and Eastern Europe.

According to these data, 37 bonds were issued in the region during 1990–98 to finance power, oil and gas, telecommunications, and rail and transportation projects. The Czech Republic leads with 23 bonds issued, 13 of which were issued by private infrastructure providers.

The volume of infrastructure bond financing during the same period was much greater in Western European countries. For the purpose of providing a perspective for the Central and Eastern European bond issues, table 12 summarizes U.S. dollar bond issues in Western Europe for 1990–98.

Table 13 presents the average risk premiums spreads on infrastructure bonds issued during 1995–98 in selected countries throughout Europe. The spreads are listed in basis point units.

Prediction of the spread as a measurement of the cost of investor risk perception might help explain the differences in the infrastructure finance approaches of the two leading transition economies.

Model Application to Estimate Risk Spreads on Czech and Hungarian Infrastructure Bonds

The resulting estimate is useful for comparing risk levels in these two countries with those of other emerging economies that have issued infrastructure bonds.

Table 11 Registered Eastern European Bond Issues, 1990–98 (All Currencies)

	Number of issues, by industry and issuer type										
	Power			Oil/gas		Railroads	Telecom				Total
Country	Issuer nationality	Central government	Public utility	Private corporate	Private utility	Private corporate	Public utility	Public corporate	Private corporate	Private finance	Private utility
Czech Rep		8	9	1	2		2	1			23
Estonia		1									1
Poland					1						1
Russia				1	2					1	4
Slovak Rep.	2			1		4					7
Total	2	9	9	3	5	4	2	1	1	1	37

Source: Euromoney Bondware.

Table 12 Registered Western European Bond Issues, 1990–98 (U.S. Dollar Issues)

	Number of issues, by industry and issuer type										
	Energy utility			*Financial corporate*		*Oil/gas*		*Telecom*			
Country	*Public utility*	*Private corporate*	*Private utility*	*Public finance*	*Private finance*	*Private corporate*	*Private utility*	*Private corporate*	*Private finance*	*Private utility*	*Total*
Austria						2	2	3			7
Germany								1			1
Denmark					1						1
Spain	1			2	2					1	6
France	3					1	2				6
Greece	1										1
Ireland								2			2
Luxembourg								1			1
Netherlands	1				5	1		4	1		12
Norway					5	4	2				11
Sweden	1										1
United Kingdom		4	12	2	14	9		27		2	70
Total	7	4	12	4	27	17	6	38	1	3	119

Source: Euromoney Bondware.

Table 13 Actual Average Spread Observations in Western and Central/Eastern European Countries, 1995–98

Country	*Average spread of public issuers*	*Average spread of private issuers*
Austria	54	105.5
Spain	54.5	71.7
France	19.25	33
Britain		70.1
Greece	145	
Netherlands	20	50
Norway	9.5	102.3
Sweden	96	
Poland		428
Slovak Republic	115	

Source: Euromoney Bondware, author's calculations.

Using the regression coefficients estimated by the spread model in Section 6, as well as actual governance and macroeconomic data, spread estimates were prepared for hypothetical bonds with a principal of US$250 million issued by Hungarian private and public sector entities in the power, oil and gas, telecommunications, and transport sectors in 1997. Similar estimates were prepared for the Czech Republic, which led Eastern and Central Europe in the number of infrastructure bond issues, as the data on actual bond spreads for the Czech Republic are not available. The results were compared with actual average spreads across the industrialized, emerging, and developing country groups.

The results of the model estimation for Hungary and the Czech Republic are shown in table 14. The aggregation of actual spread data for the three groups of countries and for the different infrastructure sectors is also shown.

Table 14 Model Estimation of Risk Spreads, Worldwide and by Country, 1997

	Mean spread of public issuers		*Mean spread of private issuers*	
Stable countries cluster	56.32	(power)	112	(power)
(actual)	28.55	(telecom)	318.53	(telecom)
Weak countries cluster	166.74	(power)	241.43	(power)
(actual)	245.58	(telecom)	313.43	(telecom)
Risky countries cluster	296.4	(power)	249.6	(power)
(actual)	394.07	(telecom)	286.67	(telecom)
Hungary	181.3	(power)	380	(power)
(estimated)	200.34	(telecom)	383.8	(telecom)
Czech Republic	130.78	(power)	272.9	(power)
(estimated)	132.16	(telecom)	275.6	(telecom)

Source: Euromoney Bondware, author's calculations.

The estimates of risk spreads on the hypothetical power and telecommunications bond issues by public and private issuers in Hungary are higher than those for the Czech Republic. They are also higher than the actual mean spreads of bonds issued in emerging economies (the "weak" countries) and of the bonds issued in most of the developing ("risky") countries. They are more than three times higher than the spreads on bonds in the developed ("stable") countries. With the exception of the estimated spread on Hungarian public telecom bonds, all estimates are greater than the actual mean spreads on bonds issued in emerging market countries. Importantly, the model evaluated private sector bond investments as very risky in Hungary, with estimated spreads on private telecommunications, power, and transport bonds being significantly higher than the average estimates of those for developing countries.

By contrast, the Czech Republic, which has been financing infrastructure through bond issues, including private ones, has risk spread estimations within the bounds of those of the emerging economies, and lower than those of Hungary.

In practice, the risk level depends on the specific circumstances of each investment, but there are also general factors—including political and regulatory factors—that determine the risk rating. These factors lift the spreads for Hungary, for which a significant portion of the spread estimate variation is attributed to governance risks. A deeper understanding of the nature of these risks in Hungary is important for the promotion of private infrastructure investment.

Industry-Level Regulatory Risks: The Cost of Regulatory Discretion

To attract private investment at reasonable cost, governments must make credible commitments to rules that safeguard property rights, provide for enforcement of contracts, and ensure transparent and stable regulation. There is no single regulatory design that can be applied to all countries to win the confidence of investors, but works by North, Levy, and Spiller (1994), Weingast (1995), and Henisz (1996) suggest that utility regulation is likely to have the greatest credibility in conjunction with political systems that restrain legislative and executive rent-seeking and opportunism. Such restraints, however, are also likely to bring about efficiency losses and higher transaction costs. The shape of regulatory institutions in a society is usually derived from the "specific institutional endowment of the nation" (Levy and Spiller, 1994),comprising its legislative and executive institutions, judicial institutions, ideology, and customs and culture, as well as the country's administrative capabilities.

This research has thus far concentrated on country-level governance risk factors. It will next address the impact on the spread of risks that stem from governmental regulation of particular industries.

Infrastructure activities are normally subject to detailed industry- or project-specific regulation, tailored to the objectives of those activities. The risk to investors arises from uncertainty over how the government will exercise its regulatory authority over the investment in order to control entry, prices, profits, and other parameters. Depending on the design of the regulatory framework, this risk might encompass one or more of three actions: (1) the exercise of discretion reserved to the government by law or contract in a manner unfavorable to the investor; (2) the amendment of laws or other unilateral regulatory instruments in a manner unfavorable to the investor; and (3) the repudiation of a specific contractual commitment on regulatory issues.

Empirically it is most plausible to attempt to discern the impact of industry-level regulations in the power sector, as this sector is characterized by distinguishable regulatory framework patterns that are common internationally. In contrast, regulation of the oil and gas and telecom sectors varies greatly from country to country, and hence is difficult to categorize for modeling purposes.

The analysis of this section is based on a set of exogenous industry characteristics, chosen as independent variables, which are likely to explain the bond credit risk. These variables include the extent of privatization, industry structure type (vertical vs. unbundled), and the ability (discretion) of a regulator to set or change prices independently of other political actors.

Ownership and structure data and information on the pricing discretion of the power sector regulators were compiled from various literature sources, including the 1999 World Energy Council survey of power sector restructuring around the world and the 1999 ESMAP Report on the Restructuring of the Electricity Industry in Developing Countries. Table 15 defines the dummy variables on which the data were compiled.

Initial correlation analysis of the relationship between these variables and the spread on power bonds revealed that the predominance of government ownership in the sector, as measured by no or limited privatization, is viewed as risky by private investors and is significantly positively correlated with the spread on power bonds.

Vertical integration of electricity utilities is negatively related to the spread, suggesting that unbundled utilities are perceived as riskier by bond investors. Without government backing, unbundled utilities do not enjoy monopolist rents and face commercial and increased political risks. To the private investor, vertically integrated monopolies appear to be a safer investment.

Table 15 Classification of Employed Power Sector Governance Framework Characteristics

Variable	*Power sector characteristics*
Extent of privatization	1, if no privatization taken place or privatization process initiated 0, if privatization substantially complete or always in private ownership
Industry structure	1, if vertically integrated industry 0, if unbundled industry or mixed structure
Regulator pricing discretion	1, if regulator can set/change prices at its own discretion (that is, does not have to follow the process of approval by other government policy institutions). 0, otherwise

Source: World Energy Council's survey and author's definitions.

It is also notable that there is a significant negative relationship between the spread and the ability of a utility regulator to set prices at its own discretion. This correlation suggests that the absence of political constraints on regulatory discretion increases the credit risk and deters investors (table 16). This phenomenon is studied in greater detail later in this section.

Instrumental Variable Approach to Regulatory Discretion Measurement

The endogeneity of the variable that indicates whether or not the power regulator has the discretion to set prices independently of other political or regulatory agencies has not been addressed by earlier research in this area. Such discretion is a function of a variety of structural and political factors. If included in the regression of the risk premium without correction for endogeneity, there is a risk that this variable will cause multicollinearity effects with other independent variables. To correct for this problem, the regulatory discretion to set prices variable was instrumentally predicted using exogenous structural societal and political variables. The estimation (prediction) was performed via instrumental variables regression (two-stage least squares regression), characterized by the system of two simultaneous equations with two endogenous variables, with regulatory pricing discretion and the spread on the left hand

Table 16 Correlation Coefficients of Power Industry Characteristics and the Log of Spread

Correlation	*Log spread*	*No privatization*	*Vertical integration*	*Regulatory discretion*
Log spread	1.00			
No privatization	.176**	1.00		
Vertical integration	-.296**	.071*	1.00	
Regulatory discretion	.287**	-.041	-.314**	1.00

Note: * – denotes significance at 10 percent level; ** – denotes significance at 5 percent level.
Source: Author's calculations.

side and exogenous macroeconomic and structural governance factor variables on the right. (Detailed specifications of the applied model are provided in Methodology Appendix 4.)

The variables used for prediction of an instrument free of the endogenous characteristics of the original regulatory pricing discretion variable include the Political Constraints Index; the BERI average macro-level regulatory risk indicator "blended" from the regulatory risks of greatest concern to infrastructure bond investors; and macroeconomic stability factors, including real GDP per capita, volume of stocks traded as a percentage of GDP, GDP growth, and the level of foreign direct investment.

To create an instrumental variable that would predict the values of an endogenous variable of regulatory pricing discretion, this variable was regressed on the above exogenous political environment characteristics. The resultant regression is based on 415 data points and has a relatively small explanatory power, explaining only about 17.1 percent of the dependent variable's variance. Both governance-related independent variables are significant and have a different impact on the predicted variable (table 17).

Regression results suggest a significant negative relationship at 95 percent level between the number of veto points (political constraints) in the political system of a country and the likelihood that the regulator has discretion to set prices for the power sector.

The variable measuring the level of country's bureaucratic quality, the risk of nationalization, the law and order tradition, and contract enforceability is also significantly negatively related with the variable of regulatory pricing discretion. (Higher values of this variable imply lower risk associated with the components of the variable.) This finding suggests that societies that have high political and regulatory stability are likely to be characterized also by the absence of absolute regulatory pricing discretion.

Table 17 Instrumental Variable for Power Sector Regulatory Discretion

Independent variable	Nonstandardized coefficients
BERI average	−.185** (.012)
Political Constraints Index	−.345**(.043)
GDP per capita	−.012 (.389)
Volume of stocks traded	−.0002 (.991)
GDP growth	−.020** (.016)
Foreign direct investment	.041**(.002)
Principal amount	−.014 (.602)
Issuer public	−.076* (.090)
Power sector structure (vertically integrated vs. unbundled/mixed)	−.128** (.025)
No privatization	−.157** (.004)
Degrees of freedom	415
R square	.171

Note: Dependent variable – Power Regulator Price Discretion (binary).
* – Denotes significance at 10 percent level; ** – denotes significance at 5 percent level. Figures in parentheses are p-values.
Source: Author's calculations.

Foreign direct investment and the volume of stocks traded as a percentage of GDP differ in their impact on the regulatory discretion variable. Specifically, larger volumes of foreign direct investment indicate an increased likelihood that the price regulator has discretion to set prices. In contrast, the volume of stocks traded has a negative relationship with the discretion variable.

Estimation of the Spread Determinants, with the Regulatory Discretion Variable Corrected for Endogeneity

The next step of this analysis estimated the regression model of the log of bond spread using the following independent variables: real GDP per capita, volume of stocks traded, foreign direct investment, principal amount of the bond, issuer public dummy, and the extent of power sector privatization and vertical integration (power sector structure). An instrumental variable estimating the discretion of the price regulator was also used (table 18).Regression was estimated on 308 data points with an R square of 0.637.

According to the regression results, all independent variables, with the exception of public issuer status and the power sector structure, have a significant relationship with a dependent variable.

The coefficients on significant variables are in most cases as expected. Specifically, for bonds issued in countries with higher GDP per capita levels, better-developed stock markets, and larger amounts of foreign direct investment, the spread is likely to be smaller. Spreads on bonds issued with larger principal amounts also tend to be lower. In countries where there has been no privatization of the power sector, bond risk premiums tend to be higher. The variable of interest—the predicted extent of the price regulator's discretion—has an increasing effect on the bond spread. This reflects a higher risk perception for bonds issued by power sector utilities, which are subject to unconstrained price regulation.

Table 18 Two-Stage Least Squares with Instrumental Variable Regression Results

Independent variable	Nonstandardized coefficients
Regulator pricing direction predicted (instrumental variable)	2.844*** (.000)
Real GDP per capita	−.067** (.011)
Principal amount	−.173** (.004)
Volume of stocks traded	−.131** (.004)
Issuer public	−.120 (.195)
Foreign direct investment	−.153*** (.000)
GDP growth	.049*** (.000)
No privatization	.352*** (.000)
Power sector structure (vertically integrated or unbundled/mixed)	.087 (.481)
Degrees of freedom	308
R square	.637

Note: Dependent variable – log of bond spread.
** – Denotes significance at 5 percent level; *** – denotes significance at 1 percent level. Figures in parentheses are p-values.
Source: Author's calculations.

Test of Applied Approach Prudence: Augmented Regression Test

An augmented regression test was conducted to test whether or not there is sufficient correlation between the disturbances to warrant estimation of regulatory pricing discretion by instrumental variables. The augmented regression was conducted by including the predicted values of the endogenous right-hand side variable (regulatory pricing discretion) as a function of all exogenous variables, in a regression of the original model of the spread (see Methodology Appendix 4). The test checks whether the coefficient on the predicted endogenous variable is significant, and if so if it justifies application of two-staged least squares regression for spread explanation through industry-level regulatory risks. Table 19 presents the results of the augmented regression test.

The results of the test indicate that the coefficient on the predicted variable for regulatory pricing discretion is significant at the 99 percent level. This allows us to conclude that the two-staged least squares with instrumental variable estimation approach was prudent.

The empirical tests of the impact of regulatory discretion on the risk perception of investors in power utility bonds provide food for thought, rather than seek to establish general truisms. On the one hand, there is a strong significant positive relationship between the variable measuring regulatory discretion and the risk premiums of power project bonds. This finding would seem to suggest that investors perceive the independent price setting capability of a regulator as an additional political hazard that increases the risk of a project. On the other hand, expert independent regulators with discretionary powers are often perceived as a better alternative to patchwork regulation provided by or with the government. While empirical results can convey information about general trends, case-by-case qualitative research is necessary to reach a full understanding of the dynamics of interaction between private investment and the regulatory regime in individual countries.

Table 19 Augmented Regression Test for Appropriateness of Instrumental Variable Approach

Independent variable	*Nonstandardized coefficients*
Regulator pricing discretion	.327*** (.001)
Regulator pricing discretion predicted (instrumental variable)	2.541*** (.000)
Real GDP per capita	−.066** (.011)
Principal	−.132** (.028)
Volume of stocks traded	−.135** (.002)
Issuer public	−.126 (.167)
Foreign direct investment	−.162*** (.000)
GDP growth	.050*** (.000)
No privatization	.370*** (.000)
Power sector structure (vertically integrated vs. unbundled/mixed)	.074 (.539)
Degrees of freedom	308
R square	.652

Note: Dependent variable – log of bond spread.
** – Denotes significance at 5 percent level; *** – denotes significance at 1 percent level. Figures in parentheses are p-values.
Source: Author's calculations.

7. True Market Perceptions of Governance Influence on Infrastructure Finance: Evidence from the Time-Series Bond Data

Risk Premium in the Secondary Market: Real Factors of Change

Conceptual Framework

Analysis of risk spreads on bonds traded in the aftermarket is important for understanding which factors are significant in bond risk pricing in real-time economic and market conditions. Analysis of aftermarket bond trading enables investigation from a different angle of the relationship between risk spread, governance, and other risk factors—that is, from the perspective of the "perfect market" judgment. It also enables comparison of the perfect market formulation of credit risk and that of the credit risk analysts of the underwriting investment banks and investment funds who priced the bonds at their issue. When bonds are traded, spreads are determined by the market, so secondary market bond spreads should therefore represent the true composition of risk factors that affect the bond over its lifetime. This section of this research paper compares the analyst-perceived and market-induced determinants of bond risk premiums in order to identify whether or not there is a systematic difference between the two.

Data Sources

This analysis uses time-series data on those bonds from the main universe (that is, bonds issued in U.S. dollars in 1990–99, as reported in the Euromoney Bondware database) that were traded in the aftermarket, as registered by the Bloomberg data vendor. The data universe encompasses 244 bonds issued in the electricity, oil, gas, and telecommunications industries of 34 countries.[17] Industry sector representation among these bonds is relatively even (table 20).

The institutional type of issuers varied. Private corporations accounted for the largest share of bonds issued (79), with private utilities (54) and public utilities (50) also accounting for a large proportion. The full breakdown of issuers is shown in table 21.

The dependent variable in this analysis is the secondary market indicative sale spread. Information on these spreads was compiled from time-series data on the semiannual yields of those main universe bonds that were traded in the aftermarket, as registered by the Bloomberg data vendor. The spreads were then calculated by taking the difference between these yields and the yields on U.S. Treasury bonds of the same maturity, as obtained through

42

Table 20 Distribution of Industry Sectors of Bond Issuers

Issuer industry	Number of issues	Percentage
Electricity	81	33.33
Financial	26	10.70
Oil/gas	61	25.10
Telecom	75	30.86
Total	243	100.00

Source: Euromoney Bondware.

Table 21 Distribution of Institutional Types of Bond Issuers

Institutional type	Number	Percentage
Central government	1	0.41
Public corporate	25	10.25
Public finance	4	1.64
Public utility	50	20.49
Subnational	5	2.05
Private corporate	79	32.38
Private financial	26	10.66
Private utility	54	22.13
Grand total	244	100.00

Source: Euromoney Bondware.

interpolation of the historical U.S. government yield curve. This exercise resulted in 26,905 weekly spread observations for the 244 bonds.

The relatively constant nature of the independent variables data (single observation for bond financial and yearly observations for macroeconomic and political/regulatory indicators) means that the time-series database could be constructed using only the annual secondary market spread observations. The dependent variable—the spread—was taken as reported in the third week of January for each year throughout the bond's life in the secondary market. To allow for delays in the information on macroeconomic, political, and regulatory risk factors leaking into the market, the independent variables observations were matched to these annual spread observations using the indicators from December of the preceding year. Bond financial characteristics were used as at issue. The resulting database of historical spread observations comprises 253 observations, with those bonds that traded for less than one year in the secondary market dropped from the sample universe.

Model Specification: Generalized Estimating Equations Model

The model chosen to test the determinants of the historical spreads uses the GEE (generalized estimating equations) population-averaged model approach, which assumes that the spread data for each bond are intercorrelated over time. Specifically, in addition to the main

43

independent variables (such as real GDP per capita, etc.) the model also includes "nuisance" variables measuring covariations between spread observations over time. There are two approaches to estimation of these nuisance variables: AR(1), which reduces the set of nuisance covariates to only one parameter; and the Robust approach, which considers as many nuisance covariates as there are different pairs of observations in the same cluster (see Methodology Appendix 5). The results obtained via these two approaches are presented in the third column of table 22.

Summary Results of Model Estimation

The results of both measurement approaches are very close, suggesting that there is little, if any, time factor estimation bias. A comparison of historical data analysis (table 22, columns 2 and 3) and cross-sectional data analysis (column 4) may be used to test for systematic difference between bond risk pricing by analysts (at issuance) and by the market (in secondary market trading):

The signs of the at-issuance and real-time coefficients are the same, with the exception of the principal amount, the higher size of which in the secondary market conditions is found to actually increase the risk of bond defaults. The impact weights of the coefficients on the spread, however, are distributed differently.

The magnitudes of all of the secondary market spread coefficients, with the important exception of the governance risk rating, are lower than those of the at-issuance spread. For example, the macroeconomic indicator of greatest importance in at-issuance risk pricing—

Table 22 Results of Historical Spread Regression

	Standardized coefficients		
Independent	*AR(1) estimation model (time series)*	*Robust estimation model (time series)*	*At-issuance spread OLS model (cross-sectional)*
Power	.165***	.183***	.256***
Oil/gas	.117**	.137**	.203***
Telecom	.108	.124	.245***
GDP growth	−.005**	−.011***	−.021
BERI	−.731***	−.752***	−.517***
Real GDP per capita	−.067**	−.037**	−.193***
Public issuer	−.090***	−.079***	−.248***
Gross foreign investment	−.109	−.104	−.005
Volume of stocks traded	.036	.034	−.166***
Principal	.099**	.124**	−.089**
R square	.653	.758	.651

Note: Dependent variable – log of bond spread.
** – Denotes significance at 5 percent level; *** – denotes significance at 1 percent level.
Source: Author's calculations.

real GDP per capita—is attributed a more modest weight by the secondary market evaluation of the risk of bond default.

More important, in the view of the market, is the rate of economic growth in the country: the significance of the coefficient on this variable has changed from less than 90 percent to 99 percent probability. The market additionally considers power sector projects to be the riskiest, with telecommunications projects carrying no additional risk, per se. In contrast to the situation at bond issuance, the volume of stocks traded has no influence whatsoever on the risk pricing of previously issued bonds. The issuance of bonds by public entities still appears to impress investors as a guarantee of safety from default.

The governance risk factor has the greatest impact on the spread, signifying that investors in off-the-run fixed income securities are even more polity- and regulatory risk-averse than the analysts pricing bonds at issuance perceive them to be.

Analysis of the interaction of the spread and mean indicators of four governance risk clusters—corruption and autocracy, fundamentalism, political disorder, and economic policy sustainability—supports the finding of earlier cross-sectional analysis on the hierarchy of these clusters (table 23).

Time-series examination of bond credit risk structure in the secondary market supports the earlier findings, with the only difference being that all four governance risk clusters have a significant effect on the secondary market spread. It is notable that when the four regulatory risk variables are taken together in the regression analysis of historical spreads, their combined power seems to crowd out the influence of other independent variables.

Table 23 Results of Historical Spread Regression, with Four Regulatory Risk Clusters

Independent variable	Nonstandardized coefficients and P-value
Power	.359 (.217)
Oil/gas	.382 (.216)
Telecom	.260 (.399)
GDP growth	−.012 (.826)
Real GDP per capita	−.073** (.050)
Public issuer	−.147 (.192)
Foreign direct investment	−.052 (.243)
Volume of stocks traded	.040 (.492)
Corruption and autocracy risk cluster average	−.996*** (.000)
Political disorder risk cluster average	−.344** (.027)
Economic policy risk cluster average	−.213*** (.000)
Fundamentalism risk cluster average	−.298** (.014)
Principal	.099**
R square	.653

Note: Dependent variable – log of historical bond spread.
** – Denotes significance at 5 percent level; *** – denotes significance at 1 percent level. Figures in parentheses are p-values.
Source: Author's calculations.

45

Regulatory Risk and Credit Rating History of Infrastructure Bonds

The fourth approach of the regulatory risk impact analysis examines the link between the governance framework and bond credit rating history. This approach is centered on the determination of if and how regulatory and political risk factors affect rating downgrades and upgrades by the major credit control agencies Standard and Poors and Moody's.

Data and Estimation Approach

This research processed the upgrade and downgrade information registered in. the Euromoney Bondware database by assigning numerical values to the letter grades issued by the two agencies and registering the date when the rating change occurred.

In order to estimate the probability of rating change, binary codes were assigned to bonds using the Rating Change (RC) variable: that is, if RC < 0, then Binary Change = -1; if RC > 0, then Binary Change = 1; otherwise 0. Using the date of rating change, a time-series database was constructed by linking these events with corresponding indicators of macroeconomic and political risk conditions. The database contains 549 observation points drawn from annual observations of the rating changes registered for 245 bonds in the Euromoney Bondware database.

The purpose of this analysis is to determine how changes in the governance regime and macroeconomic and firm conditions affect the decision of the rating agencies to alter the credit rating of issued bonds, and therefore indirectly the risk price of infrastructure bonds, as measured by the spreads. The analysis used the multinomial logit technique for three outcomes, which enables estimation of the probability that an observation belongs to one of the three observation groups: (-1) downgrade; (0) no change; and (1) upgrade. (Detailed specifications of the multinomial logit model can be found in Methodology Appendix 6.)

Results of Model Estimation

The results of the multinomial logit regression suggest that changes in governance conditions, stock market growth, gross foreign direct investment, real GDP per capita, GDP growth, and firm-intrinsic risk factors significantly affect the decision made by the major rating agencies to change a rating (table 24).

Analysis of the multinomial regression results segregate the factors of credit rating stability from the factors of credit rating change (both positive and negative). According to this analysis, GDP per capita, gross FDI, and the industry sector dummies are variables capable of inducing credit rating change. Specifically, an increase in GDP per capita has a positive significant influence (at 95 percent level) on the probability of a bond being upgraded, but no influence whatsoever on the probability of downgrade. Positive changes in the power and oil and gas sector firm-intrinsic conditions have a significant negative influence on the probability of a bond being downgraded, with negative changes accordingly increasing the downgrade probability of the bond. GFDI has a positive significant impact on the probability of a

Table 24 Multinomial Logit Regression Results

Independent variables	Nonstandardized coefficients and P-value	
	Probability to belong to (–1)	*Probability to belong to (1)*
BERI average (governance risk)	–4.796* (.057)	–7.347** (.008)
Volume of stocks traded	2.073* (.053)	1.866* (.067)
Foreign direct investment	1.879** (.039)	–.013 (.992)
Real GDP per capita	–.115 (.813)	2.163** (.005)
GDP growth	–.343** (.007)	–.513*** (.000)
Power dummy	–5.995** (.014)	–.329 (.698)
Oil and gas dummy	–4.067* (.082)	–.811 (.437)
Issuer public dummy	.258 (.779)	.211 (.812)
Principal amount	–.001 (.645)	–.001 (.651)
Constant	2.262 (.678)	–10.959 (.019)
Summary statistics	Pseudo R2: 0.371	Number of observations: 332

Note: * – denotes significance at 10 percent level; ** – denotes significance at 5 percent level; *** – denotes significance at 1 percent level. Figures in parentheses are p-values.
Source: Author's calculations.

bond being downgraded, a finding that might be explained by the increased competition to existing investments that accompanies a rise in FDI.

The second set of significant independent variables—the BERI average, measuring political and regulatory risks, and GDP growth—serve as factors of credit rating stability. Specifically, both the greater rate of GDP growth and the higher level of governance stability have a negative impact on both the probability of a bond being upgraded or downgraded. Essentially, this signifies that a large increase in political and regulatory stability in a country decreases the volatility of credit rating change; a decrease in the quality of governance is conversely likely to bring about instability in bond credit ratings. Changes in GDP growth affect a similar pattern of change on bond ratings.

Finally, the volume of stocks traded variable acts as a mirror reflection of the regulatory and growth variables. An increase in the volume of stocks traded has a positive significant effect on the probability of a rating upgrade or downgrade. This can be attributed to the link between a rise in a country's trading profile and the amount of attention that rating agencies pay to its market.

The findings of this section allow us to conclude that governance frameworks, and specifically the associated presence or absence of political and regulatory risks, are crucial factors at the initiation of private infrastructure bond financing. Once financing has been attracted, even major improvements in the quality of governance are unlikely to affect the credibility of an investment and the cost of borrowed funds. In summary, good governance is instrumental in attracting and initiating private investment in infrastructure.

8. Conclusions

The purpose of this paper has been to investigate the nature of interaction between the quality of governance and the risks facing private infrastructure investment. The following aspects of governance were examined: (1) democratic development; (2) efficiency of the bureaucracy; (3) enforcement of the law and of contracts; (4) the transparency of and corruption in government activities; (5) traditional political risks of war, coups, expropriation, and tendency toward dictatorship, as evidenced by organized religion or the presence of the military in government; and (6) industry-level regulation. Macroeconomic, bond, and industry sector characteristics were also included in the analysis, thereby expanding upon earlier models examining credit risk. The main research findings are as follows:

First, the research confirmed the hypothesis that governance risk has a substantial impact on the risk of default on a fixed-income security issued to finance infrastructure projects. Different political and regulatory risks were additionally found to have nonhomogeneous impacts on the bond spread: cluster analysis segregated an array of risk indicators into four groups, categorized as risks of (1) political disorder; (2) corruption, red tape, and autocracy; (3) poor economic policy; and (4) fundamentalism.

Empirical evidence suggests that what matters most to investors are the risks of corruption, poor bureaucratic quality (red tape), and the lack of institutional constraints preventing adverse governmental action (autocracy). Second in the hierarchy of importance are the traditional risks of political disorder, as manifested by civil war, military control of politics, political terrorism, the absence of a tradition of law and order, and nationalization policies. Investors appear to be least susceptible to risks that stem from shortsighted economic policies and poor planning, and to fundamentalism risks such as those manifested by the prevalence of organized religion in politics, internal racial and nationality tensions, and the risk of external conflict.

In other words, investors are prepared to diversify away a fair amount of incompetence in political and economic leadership, and also of inconsistency in economic policy. Empirically, it appears that poor political leadership and economic mismanagement are increasingly being seen as diversifiable incompetence and no longer as a systemic threat to investors. Investors are also prepared to deal with differences in the cultural and moral endowments of a country; they are not, however, prepared to risk the hazards that stem from systemic incentives to steal (corruption) or to break commitments (poor contract enforceability). These latter factors reduce expected values and require an offsetting spread.

The findings on the importance hierarchy of the four risk clusters was reinforced by the results of a time-series examination of bond credit risk structure in the secondary market. The only major difference in these results was that all four governance risk clusters had a significant effect on the secondary market spread. Spreads in the aftermarket essentially measure the monetary compensation for a bond's risk of default, as dictated by real market risk judgement, as opposed to bond spreads at-issuance, which are determined by the risk judgement of analysts from underwriting banks and institutional investment entities.

Second, the research identified a clear separation of the countries of the sample universe into three regulatory and political risk clusters, characterized by stable, weak, and risky governance climates. To a large extent, these groups to a large extent mirror what the development community conventionally calls the "worlds" of industrialized, emerging, and developing economies. Members of the risky governance cluster[18]—the least developed countries and those countries struggling in transition—generally have very poor governance as well as poor macroeconomic indicators, and consequently have to pay high premiums to investors for taking on the risk of investment in such an environment.

Countries in the weak cluster[19]—the emerging economies—were successful in setting some of the fiscal, monetary policy, and ownership structure fundamentals right. Governance issues nonetheless remain their toughest challenge, as they have to resolve the issues that give rise to a whole range of political and regulatory risks. According to the estimates of this research, the price that infrastructure bond issuers paid in 1997 to cover the risks of corruption, red tape, and poor law enforcement was extremely high, amounting to otherwise avoidable spread payments of $697.7 million. These are the funds that could have been saved by the sponsors of infrastructure projects in emerging markets if the governments of those markets had been able to offer risk-free governance. Although these are subjective estimates, and reflect the inherent subjectivity of governance risk ratings, it is clear that poor policies and weak governance frameworks are extremely costly and that they impede the development both of needed infrastructure and of capital markets. Other factors dictating bond spreads in these countries include the extent of capital market development, as measured by the volume of stocks traded as a percentage of GDP, and the overall macroeconomic stability, as measured by real GDP per capita. Higher values of these variables have a decreasing effect on infrastructure bond spreads.

As a case study, the research applied the model developed here to estimate the expected risk return for infrastructure investors in two transition economies, the Czech Republic and Hungary, in 1997. The Czech Republic notably issued more infrastructure bonds than any other Central and Eastern European country; Hungary, in contrast, preferred other types of infrastructure financing. The model estimation indicated that the cost of borrowing in Hungary should be higher and in the Czech Republic lower than the actual average spread for emerging market countries in that year, in order to compensate potential investors for the political and regulatory risks that they would face. This may partly explain the difference in the two countries' choices of infrastructure finance sources.

Members of the stable cluster of countries[20]—the industrialized economies—are in the clear. The risk premiums of bonds issued in the political and regulatory environments of these countries were found to include no component reflecting governance risk. Investors in these countries are free to concern themselves exclusively with real commercial project risk, rather than with policy risk created by the adverse actions of government. Risk spreads are predominantly determined by firm-, project-, and industry sector-intrinsic characteristics, as measured in this analysis by industry sector dummies. Another important factor is the institutional type of bond issuer. The association of the bond issue with the public sector has a strong decreasing effect on the bond spread, as investors perceive this to be a sign of state underwriting of the project in the event of bond default. Interestingly, public sector association has little effect in the case of emerging markets, where investors perceive government commitments to be unreliable. The conclusion that may be drawn from these findings is that economic reform remains a necessary but not a sufficient approach to development.

Third, the research found a substantial degree of variation in the impact of regulatory and political risks on the spread for bond issuers according to their institutional and ownership characteristics. There is clear evidence of asymmetry in the extent of exposure to adverse government action that are faced by the different ownership types of infrastructure bonds. Specifically, private sector infrastructure projects were found to be systemically more vulnerable to the effect of political and regulatory risks than were public sector projects, and more so in the emerging market countries.

Fourth, this research studied on an international level the effects of risks posed by industry structure and regulation. Examination of the risk premium structure of bonds issued for the financing of power sector projects the research found that there is a fine line between the benefits bestowed by regulatory independence and the hazards, as perceived by investors, that potentially stem from the same granting of regulatory discretion—particularly in regard to pricing. Specifically, the research found that the absence of political constraints on a regulator's ability to set prices significantly increases the investment risk, as measured by the bond spread. Low levels of power sector privatization were also found to increase investor risk perceptions. These findings highlight a need for the careful assessment of the pros and cons when regulatory reform is undertaken and of the extent of independence afforded to regulators.

Fifth, the project investigated the structure of risk spread from a new angle—that is, from the perspective of a "perfect market" judgement. It investigated whether or not the perfect market formulation of credit risk is different from that of the analysts who set bond pricing at issuance. The results of time-series data analysis revealed that market risk perceptions deviate slightly from those of credit risk analysts at bond issuance in two aspects only. While regulatory and political risks remain an important and significant factor in the investor's risk perception over the bond's lifetime in the secondary market, macroeconomic conditions diminish in importance, with the single exception of the rate of economic growth, which has a significant decreasing effect on the bond risk spread.

Finally, study of the credit rating history of the bonds universe enabled discernment between the factors of an investment's creditworthiness stability and the factors of creditworthiness change. Stable governance frameworks were found to be essential for credit rating stability, but firm-intrinsic factors wielded the greatest influence over changes in credit agency ratings. This suggests that governance frameworks are crucial factors at the initiation of private infrastructure bond financing. Once financing has been attained, even major improvements in the quality of governance are unlikely to affect the credit rating of borrowed funds. Good governance may be construed therefore as instrumental primarily for attracting and initiating private investment in infrastructure, and for maintenance of stable rates.

Overall, this research provided empirical evidence that international governance conditions are a significant factor determining the flow of private finance to and the cost of borrowing for infrastructure. It also points to the need for future work to include a deeper qualitative analysis of governance frameworks and of their associated political and regulatory risks, ideally on a case-by-case basis and including examination of the ways in which changes might be introduced into governance frameworks to provide better conditions for private infrastructure financing.

Methodology Appendix 1.
The Mathematical Foundation of Biplot Analysis[21]

0.   Fact: any *nxm* matrix Y of rank r can be factorized (non-uniquely!) as a product

$$Y = GH' \tag{1}$$

into an *n by r* matrix G and *mxr* matrix H

1.   Let us first assume an unrealistic case, that the *n by m* data matrix Y is exactly of rank 2, then using (1) any data entry $y_{i,j}$ can be represented without loss of information as an inner product of the corresponding two vectors $g_i{}'$ and h_j from matrices G and H, that is

$$y_{ij} = g_i' h_j \tag{2}$$

By this factorization we assign 2-dimensional vectors $g_1, g_2, ..., g_n$ to the rows of the original data matrix Y and 2-dimensional vectors $h_1, h_2, ..., h_m$ for the *m* columns of Y.

2.   Now we can plot this $n + m$ vectors on the two-dimensional plane, giving the representation of the *mn* elements of matrix Y by means of the inner products of the corresponding row effect and column effect vectors. Such a plot was originally referred to as *biplot* in Gabrilel (71) as it allows the row effects and column effects to be plotted jointly.

3.   In terms of the *graphical interpretation*, the inner product of the two vectors g and h can be appraised visually by considering it as a product of the length of one of the vectors times the length of the other vector's projection onto it. This allows one to see easily which rows or columns in the matrix Y are proportional to which rows or columns (same directions); which entries are zero (right angles between rows and columns) and so forth.

4.   Now consider an arbitrary *n by m* data matrix Y or rank $r \leq \min(n,m)$. The idea is first to construct a rank 2 approximation of any such matrix or rank r (denoted as $Y_{(2)}$) and then to use the biplot of this rank 2 matrix as a visual representation of the original matrix Y. Obviously, the usefulness of this biplot would depend on the quality of this approximation, that is on the distance $\| Y - Y_{(2)} \|$.

5. To approximate any rectangular *n by m* matrix Y of rank *r* by *n by m* matrix of a lower rank we can use the *singular value decomposition* technique. That is, we can represent Y as

$$Y = \sum_{i=1}^{r} \lambda_i \, p_i \, q_i' \qquad (3)$$

where

- λ_i is the square root of the *i*-th eigenvalue of the squared matrix $Y'Y$ and $0 \le \lambda_r \dots \le \lambda_2 \le \lambda_1$
- q_i is the *i*-th eigenvector of the squared matrix $Y'Y$
- p_i is the *i*-th eigenvector of the squared matrix YY'

6. Now let us take as a two-rank approximation:

$$Y_{(2)} = \sum_{i=1}^{2} \lambda_i \, p_i \, q_i'. \qquad (4)$$

It has been proven that such constructed matrix $Y_{(2)}$ would minimize the squared norm

$$\|Y - M\| = \sum_{i=1}^{n} \sum_{j=1}^{m} (y_{ij} - m_{ij})^2 \qquad (5)$$

with respect to M. Furthermore, the extent of lack of fit is measured by the sum of the eigenvalues corresponding to the higher dimensions:

$$\|Y - Y_{(2)}\| = \lambda_3^2 + \lambda_4^2 \dots + \lambda_r^2. \qquad (6)$$

7. The *principal component biplot* now is defined as follows: An *n by m* data matrix Y is considered, in which the mean of each variable has been subtracted out. Then $Y'Y/n = S$, the covariance matrix. The data can be further standardized by dividing each column by the corresponding standard deviation. In the latter case, $Y'Y/n = R$, the correlation matrix. Now consider rank 2 approximation $Y_{(2)}$ for biplotting with $G = (p_1, p_2)\sqrt{n}$ and $H = (\lambda_1 q_1, \lambda_2 q_2) / \sqrt{n}$, then we can observe that the following approximate relationships hold:

$$\begin{aligned} Y &\sim GH' \\ YS^{-1}Y' &\sim GG' \qquad (7) \\ S &\sim HH' \end{aligned}$$

That is,

- The data entries $y_{i,j}$ would be represented by the inner products of the corresponding vectors g, h; therefore one can gain a rough idea about the distribution of low, medium, and high values of different variables by looking at the biplot.
- The standardized distance between i and i' observations is approximated by

$$d(i,i') = \left(y_i - y_{i'} \right)' S^{-1} \left(y_i - y_{i'} \right) = \left\| g_i - g_{i'} \right\|. \tag{8}$$

Therefore the Euclidean distances between the points representing the observations on the biplot approximate the differences between the observations in the underlying multidimensional space; furthermore, by projecting the multidimensional observations onto a plane we can easily detect clusters of observations with similar values for all variables.

- The covariances between the variables of the data set are represented by the inner products of the corresponding column vectors h, and the correlations correspond to the cosines of the angles between these vectors (when the data are standardized, both measures coincide, as all column vectors are of the same unit length).

8.   As has been emphasized, the quality of the biplot representation can be judged based on the *goodness of fit* criterion, and its values being close to unity would indicate a very good approximation.

$$\rho = \frac{\lambda_1^2 + \lambda_2^2}{\sum\limits_{i=1}^{r} \lambda_i^2} \tag{9}$$

Methodology Appendix 2.
OLS Spread Model for Cross-Sectional Data: Macro-Level Regulatory Risks Impact Measurement

This section uses an augmented multifactor logistic risk spread model to analyze the determinants of the yield spread on bonds. This model, in variations, has been used by Edwards (1986), Angbazo and others (1996), and Eichengreen and Mody (1997) to study different aspects of the formation processes of bond and loan spreads. Here, we assume that yield spreads on bonds under consideration are determined as follows:

Model 1

$$\log(S_{it}) = F(X_{it}) + \varepsilon_{it}$$

The dependent variable is defined as the logarithm of the spread S_{it} over a benchmark (U.S. Treasury) of bonds issued to finance infrastructure projects in country i in year t. X_{it} is the vector of independent variables, which will be used to measure how the credit risk premium is related to a set of explanatory variables. Log of spread is a traditional measure of risk premium that bond issuers have to pay investors for undertaken risk of a principal and interest loss.

The data of this research (described in the following section) are contemporaneous and were compiled in a rectangular table with columns representing variables and rows representing distinct projects. To specify the model further, each bond will have a country index ($c = 1 \ldots N_c$) and a sector index ($s = 1 \ldots N_s$) to track to which country or sector the bond belongs. In this table, the values for each countrywide regulatory risk factor variable would be the same for all projects within the same country, and the values for each sector–specific regulatory risk factor variable would be the same for all projects in the same sector in the same country. Denoting country-wide macroeconomic performance variables by $C^{(l)}$, $l = 1 ,\ldots, l_c$, regulatory risk variables by $R^{(l)}$, $l = 1,\ldots, l_s$, and financial bond-specific variables by $P^{(l)}$, $l = 1,\ldots, l_p$, Model 1 is further elaborated:

Model 1.1

$$\log(S_i) = a + \sum_{l=1}^{l_c} \varphi_l C_i^{(l)} + \sum_{l=1}^{l_s} \phi_l R_i^{(l)} + \sum_{l=1}^{l_p} \psi_l P_i^{(l)} + other\ factors + \varepsilon_i$$

where $i = 1, \ldots, p$, p is the number of projects, and *other factors* are explanatory variables not included above (in case there are unaccounted-for fixed country or sector effects.

Model 1.1 accounts for effects of all three types (macroeconomic, political-regulatory, and financial-project) of risk variables that, according to research hypotheses, affect the spread.

Methodology Appendix 3.
Test for Universe Selection Bias—Truncated Regression

The econometric technique of truncated regression is utilized to test the presence of a selectivity bias in the data universe (sample). For example, in this research there is concern that our universe of bonds is potentially a biased sample. The basis for this concern could be that the bonds forming the research universe by default have had issuance conditions, under which quality is specified as not worse than a certain acceptable threshold. In other words, bonds in environments that are too risky have never been issued.

The method of truncated regression relies on the assumption that "successful" projects are those where $Y < c$, where Y is the spread and c is a "threshold" that can be interpreted as a maximum spread (serving as an investment environment risk indicator) allowable for a project to be financed through a bond issue. There are three model specifications of the truncated regression approach. The first one is rather complicated and supposes that the unobservable threshold is stochastic and depends on the set of explanatory variables X used in our model for Y; that is, $c = f(X) + \varepsilon$, for each observation i. The estimation of an unobserved threshold c is conducted simultaneously with the regression coefficients of the fitted model for Y via the maximum likelihood estimation. The second approach assumes that there is a single (unobservable) threshold that is the same for all cases.[22] The third approach is similar to the second but in addition contains a simplifying assumption that the threshold is a known constant.[23] Mathematical formulation of this approach is attached in Annex B of this paper. A value of 7 was chosen as a constant threshold amount for the log of spread as all values of log spreads in the research bond universe were below that number. Should the selection bias be strong, the truncated regression would result in coefficients of significantly larger magnitude.

The likelihood function for the last, more feasible approach, would be as follows:

$$\log L = -N \log\left[(2\pi)^{\frac{1}{2}}\sigma\right] - \frac{1}{2}\sum_{i=1}^{n}\left(\frac{y_i - \beta x_i}{\sigma}\right)^2 - \sum_{i=1}^{n}\log \phi\left(\frac{\mu - \beta x_i}{\sigma}\right)^2 \tag{1}$$

where $\Phi()$ is the c.d.f of the normal distribution, μ a known constant such that all values of spread higher than M were eliminated from the study, and σ is the standard deviation of the underlying normal distribution. In practice, m can be set as a number bigger than the maximum log spread observed in the sample. The estimates of the parameters β and σ are obtained by maximizing the loglikelihood with respect to those parameters. This can be done, for example, by solving the nonlinear system of equations

$$\frac{\partial \log L}{\partial \beta} = 0, \frac{\partial \log L}{\partial \sigma} = 0 \tag{2}$$

using the Newton-Raphson method or method of scoring. An alternative way to choose μ would be to consider it an unknown parameter as in approach 2 and estimate it from the data. However, the stability of the estimates and its properties has not been yet studied extensively and there is some concern in the literature.

Methodology Appendix 4.
Instrumental Variables and Two-Staged Least Squares Regression for Industry-Level Regulatory Risks Impact Measurement

1. *Instrumental Variable Model.* The estimation (prediction) was performed via the instrumental variables regression (or two-stage least squares regression) characterized by the system of two simultaneous equations with two endogenous variables—the regulatory pricing discretion and the spread on the left-hand side, and exogenous macroeconomic and structural governance factor variables on the right.

$$\begin{cases} R_{ij}\alpha_0 + \alpha_1 B_{ij} + \alpha_2 P_{ij} + \sum_{k=1}^{n} \gamma_k M_{ij}^k + \varepsilon_{ij} \\ \log(S_{ij}) = \beta_0 + \beta_1 R_{ij} + \sum_{k=1}^{n} \zeta_k M_{ij}^k + \sum_{k=1}^{m} \eta_k \phi_{ij}^k + \upsilon_{ij} \, . \end{cases} \quad (1)$$

Where i, j identify country and year of bond issue;
n, m – number of macroeconomic and bond financial factors,
S_{ij} – spread over the benchmark
R_{ij} – regulatory pricing discretion variable
B_{ij} – BERI average (macro-level regulatory risk)
P_{ij} – Political Constraints Index
M_{ij} – macroeconomic risk factors variables
Φ_{ij} – bond financial risk factor variables

The linear regression model is estimated using instrumental variables of log spread on exogenous macroeconomic variables and on the endogenous regulatory pricing discretion variable, for which in turn the exogenous governance factors such as BERI average and the Political Constraints Index are used as instrumental variables.

2. *Augmented Regression Test.* The augmented regression test was conducted to test whether or not there is significant correlation between the disturbances of the two equations so as to warrant estimation of regulatory pricing discretion by the two stage least squares. The test is performed under the assumption that the instrumental variables estimates are consistent. The augmented regression is formed by including the predicted values of the endogenous variable regulatory pricing discretion, R, as a function of all exogenous variables, in a regression of the original model of the spread. The model for augmented regression test therefore looks as follows:

$$\log(S_{ij}) = \beta_0 + \beta_1 R_{ij} + \beta_2 \hat{R}_{ij} + \sum_{k=1}^{n} \zeta_k M_{ij}^k + \sum_{k=1}^{m} \eta_k \phi_{ij}^k + \upsilon_{ij} \, . \quad (2)$$

one (parameter), ρ (of course, we have to estimate σ). At the other extreme, one can consider as many nuisance covariates as there are different pairs of observations in the same cluster, and estimate them from the data. The second estimation approach, which allows accommodation of the time factor in the spread model, is the GEE population-averaged model with the Robust estimator of the variance-covariance matrix. For estimation, the *xtgee* routine in STATA software was used. Several types of correlation patterns were tried: *exchangeable* (all same), *AR(1)* (first order autocorrelation), and *unstructured*. The results of these routines were very similar, which is consistent with some theoretical and simulation results that state that the analysis in GEE is robust to the mild deviation in the independent errors.

Methodology Appendix 6.
Multinomial Logit Technique for Estimation of the Probability of the Bond Credit Rating Change

The multinomial logit technique allows us to estimate the probabilities that an observation belongs to any of the k groups—in our case, (–1) downgrade; (0) no change; and (1) upgrade.

This research exploited the multinomial logit model for $k = 3$ outcomes (which is an extension of the usual logistic regression with $k = 2$ outcomes) to simultaneously estimate the set of equations:

$$\Pr\left(y_{ij} = 1 \mid x_i\right) = p_i^{(j)} = \frac{\exp\left(z_i^{(j)}\right)}{1 + \exp\left(z_i^{(2)}\right) + \exp\left(z_i^{(3)}\right)}, j = 2,\ldots 3$$

$$z_i^{(j)} = a^{(j)} x_i, j = 2,3 \quad i = 1,\ldots n \tag{1}$$

where y's are the set of binary response variables:
$y_{ij} = 1$ if the bond i belongs to the group j, and
$y_{ij} \, y_{ij} = 0$; otherwise x_i is the vector of explanatory variables for the i-th bond, and
n is total number of bonds.

One of the k groups (here it is the middle, 0 or no change) has to be fixed as a *reference group* (or base category). This means that the coefficients of the corresponding equation must be all set to zero, so that we actually estimate the set of k-1 equations, which in the case of a regular logit model with two groups reduces to a single equation with coefficients $\{a_0, a_1, a_2, \ldots a_m\}$.

It can be easily shown then, that $\exp(z_i^{(j)})$ expresses the probability that the bond i belongs to a group (j), **relative** to the probability that it belongs to the reference category (here the reference category is the *no-change* group), namely:

$$\exp\left(z_i^{(j)}\right) = \Pr\left(y_i = j\right) / \Pr\left(y_i = 1\right). \tag{2}$$

Annex A

Table A.1 Correlation Analysis of Data Interrelationships—Correlation Clusters

	Economic expectat.	Econ. plan. fail	Political leader	External conflict	Organized religion	Racial and nationality tensions	Corrupt gov-nt	Political party	Quality of bureau	Bureac delays	Contract enforc	Nation. risk	Infra quality	Corrup Percep Index	Military in politics	Law/ order tradin	Polit. terror	Civil war risks	Polit risk rating
Economic expectations	1.00	0.87	0.69	0.04	0.16	0.21	0.33	0.23	0.39	0.49	0.48	0.56	0.47	0.35	0.35	0.38	0.41	0.32	0.57
Econ. Plan. Fail	0.87	1.00	0.71	0.19	0.20	0.25	0.33	0.31	0.32	0.43	0.45	0.52	0.38	0.26	0.30	0.31	0.28	0.21	0.56
Political leader	0.69	0.71	1.00	0.26	0.05	0.22	0.33	0.34	0.25	0.36	0.38	0.40	0.33	0.21	0.33	0.47	0.48	0.42	0.59
External conflict	0.04	0.19	0.26	1.00	0.36	0.39	0.18	0.44	0.16	0.26	0.24	0.22	0.16	0.17	0.23	0.24	0.25	0.25	0.43
Organized religion	0.16	0.20	0.05	0.36	1.00	0.62	0.51	0.49	0.48	0.57	0.49	0.36	0.48	0.48	0.52	0.49	0.56	0.39	0.67
Racial and nationality tensions	0.21	0.25	0.22	0.39	0.62	1.00	0.24	0.24	0.12	0.33	0.26	0.29	0.21	0.22	0.33	0.25	0.49	0.23	0.51
Corrupt government	0.33	0.33	0.33	0.18	0.51	0.24	1.00	0.78	0.82	0.83	0.82	0.61	0.79	0.76	0.76	0.78	0.56	0.56	0.83
Political party	0.23	0.31	0.34	0.44	0.49	0.24	0.78	1.00	0.76	0.79	0.77	0.65	0.74	0.69	0.60	0.66	0.40	0.53	0.77
Quality of bureaucracy	0.39	0.32	0.25	0.16	0.48	0.12	0.82	0.76	1.00	0.85	0.87	0.73	0.84	0.77	0.66	0.78	0.44	0.58	0.78
Bureaucratic delays	0.49	0.43	0.36	0.26	0.57	0.33	0.83	0.79	0.85	1.00	0.95	0.81	0.92	0.86	0.68	0.77	0.54	0.54	0.85
Contract enforcement	0.48	0.45	0.38	0.24	0.49	0.26	0.82	0.77	0.87	0.95	1.00	0.87	0.91	0.84	0.69	0.81	0.52	0.57	0.84
Infrastructure quality	0.47	0.38	0.33	0.16	0.48	0.21	0.79	0.74	0.84	0.92	0.91	0.78	1.00	0.79	0.64	0.73	0.46	0.50	0.77
Corruption Perception Index	0.35	0.26	0.21	0.17	0.48	0.22	0.76	0.69	0.77	0.86	0.84	0.75	0.79	1.00	0.58	0.70	0.47	0.57	0.71
Military in politics	0.35	0.30	0.33	0.23	0.52	0.33	0.76	0.60	0.66	0.68	0.69	0.51	0.64	0.58	1.00	0.74	0.69	0.61	0.81
Nation. risk	0.56	0.52	0.40	0.22	0.36	0.29	0.61	0.65	0.73	0.81	0.87	1.00	0.78	0.75	0.51	0.66	0.42	0.50	0.72
Law/order tradin	0.38	0.31	0.47	0.24	0.49	0.25	0.78	0.66	0.78	0.77	0.81	0.66	0.73	0.70	0.74	1.00	0.73	0.81	0.87
Polit. terror	0.41	0.28	0.48	0.25	0.56	0.49	0.56	0.40	0.44	0.54	0.52	0.42	0.46	0.47	0.69	0.73	1.00	0.58	0.78
Civil war risk	0.32	0.21	0.42	0.25	0.39	0.23	0.56	0.53	0.58	0.54	0.57	0.50	0.50	0.57	0.61	0.81	0.58	1.00	0.72
Polit risk rating	0.57	0.56	0.59	0.43	0.67	0.51	0.83	0.77	0.78	0.85	0.84	0.72	0.77	0.71	0.81	0.87	0.78	0.72	1.00

Source: Author's calculations.

Annex B

Table B.1 OLS Regression of Log of Spread on Individual Regulatory Risk Factors

	Name of the tested regulatory risk									
Variable name	*Economic expectations vs. realities*	*Economic planning failures*	*Political leadership*	*External conflict*	*Corruption in government*	*Military in politics*	*Organized religion in politics*	*Law and order tradition*	*Racial/ nationality tensions*	*Political terrorism*
Foreign direct invest.	.125*** (.005)	.130*** (.005)	.134*** (.003)	.134*** (.002)	.123*** (.004)	.134*** (.003)	.129*** (.004)	.130*** (.003)	.112** (.016)	.121*** (.007)
Principal	–.099** (.016)	–.100 ** (.015)	–.102** (.014)	–.105*** (.010)	–.108*** (.006)	–.103** (.012)	–.100** (.015)	–.100** (0.014)	–.099** (.016)	–.096** (.019)
Real GDP	–.418*** (.000)	–.404*** (.000)	–.398*** (.000)	–.406*** (.000)	–.328*** (.000)	–.422*** (.000)	–.402*** (.000)	–.305*** (.000)	–.397*** (.000)	–.373*** (.000)
GDP growth	.076 * (.076)	.083 * (.056)	.089*** (.044)	–.079** (.060)	–.001 (.974)	.092** (.038)	.079* (.064)	.055 (.201)	.099** (.029)	.099** (.027)
Stocks traded	–.406 *** (.000)	–.389 *** (.000)	–.385*** (.000)	–.377*** (.000)	–.302*** (.000)	–.404*** (.000)	–.393*** (.000)	–.343*** (.000)	–.409*** (.000)	–.394*** (.000)
Regulatory risk	.042 (.340)	–.009 (.844)	–.027 (.540)	–.081** (.032)	–.245*** (.000)	.044 (.395)	–.011 (.781)	–.173*** (.006)	–.048 .263	–.066 (.151)
Public sector	–.223 *** (.000)	–.216*** (.000)	–.214*** (.000)	–.214*** (.000)	–.228*** (.000)	–.215*** (.000)	–.219*** (.000)	–.240*** (.000)	–.216*** (.000)	–.226*** (.000)
Power sector	.256*** (.000)	.258*** (.000)	.263*** (.000)	.262*** (.000)	.278*** (.000)	.265*** (.000)	.259*** (.000)	.248*** (.000)	.246*** (.000)	.271*** (.000)
Oil or gas sector	.252*** (.000)	.257*** (.000)	.262*** (.000)	.253*** (.000)	.240*** (.000)	.257*** (.000)	.259*** (.000)	.228*** (.000)	.251*** (.000)	.268*** (.000)
Telecom sector	.248*** (.000)	.248*** (.000)	.252*** (.000)	.254*** (.000)	.242*** (.000)	.251*** (.000)	.248*** (.000)	.246*** (.000)	.246*** (.000)	.263*** (.000)
Df	307	307	307	307	307	307	307	307	307	307
R Square	.590	.589	.589	.595	.620	.590	.589	.599	.590	.591

Note: Dependent variable – log of historical bond spread; * – denotes significance at 10 percent level; ** – denotes significance at 5 percent level; *** – denotes significance at 1 percent level. Figures in parentheses are p–values.
Source: Author's calculations.

Table B.2 OLS Regression of Log of Spread on Individual Regulatory Risk Factors

Variable name	Quality of the bureaucracy	ICRG composite regulatory risk rating	Bureaucratic delays	Contract enforceability	Nationalization risk	Communication/ transport infra. quality	TI Corruption Perceptions Index	Civil war	Political party development
					Name of the tested regulatory risk				
Foreign direct invest.	.028** (.022)	.128*** (.003)	.089** (.041)	.108** (.015)	.028 (.606)	–.027 (.571)	.156*** (.000)	.133*** (.003)	.121*** (.005)
Principal	–.098** (.014)	–.095 ** (.019)	–.095** (.016)	–.100** (.013)	–.101** (.013)	–.112*** (.004)	–.094** (.017)	–.099** (.016)	–.093** (.019)
Real GDP	–.335*** (.000)	–.292*** (.000)	–.225*** (.000)	–.261*** (.000)	–.291*** (.000)	–.258*** (.000)	–.283*** (.000)	–.381*** (.000)	–.231*** (.000)
GDP growth	.003 (.947)	.081* (.051)	.013 (.770)	–.003 (.947)	.083** (.050)	–.076* (.098)	.023 (.595)	.083** (.050)	.057 (.161)
Stocks traded	–.282 *** (.000)	–.389*** (.000)	–.229*** (.000)	–.260*** (.000)	–.339*** (.000)	–.099* (.095)	–.286*** (.000)	–.380*** (.000)	–.386*** (.000)
Regulatory risk	.248*** (.000)	–.182*** (.003)	–.382*** (.000)	–.301*** (.000)	–.240*** (.000)	–.536*** (.000)	–.269*** (.000)	–.047 (.370)	–.265*** (.000)
Public sector	–.246 *** (.000)	–.227*** (.000)	–.234*** (.000)	–.246*** (.000)	–.230*** (.000)	–.215*** (.000)	–.251*** (.000)	–.225*** (.000)	–.246*** (.000)
Power sector	.245*** (.000)	.250*** (.000)	.224*** (.000)	.249*** (.000)	.256*** (.000)	.258*** (.000)	.285*** (.000)	.269*** (.000)	.210*** (.001)
Oil or gas sector	.228*** (.000)	.249*** (.000)	.196*** (.001)	.224*** (.000)	.235*** (.000)	.214*** (.000)	.245*** (.000)	.262*** (.000)	.189*** (.002)
Telecom sector	.229*** (.000)	.246*** (.000)	.221*** (.000)	–.246*** (.000)	.259*** (.000)	.228*** (.000)	.256*** (.000)	.256*** (.000)	.213*** (.000)
Df	307	307	297	297	297	297	307	307	307
R Square	.614	.601	.631	.614	.609	.648	.618	.590	**Missed**

Note: Dependent variable – log of historical bond spread; * – denotes significance at 10 percent level; ** – denotes significance at 5 percent level; *** – denotes significance at 1 percent level. Figures in parentheses are p–values.
Source: Author's calculations.

Annex C

Table C.1 Definitions of Bond Issue Characteristics

Indicator	Definition
Yield to maturity (annual)	The annual rate of return on a security if held to maturity
Underwriting risk period	The number of days (inclusive) between pricing date and offer date
Same guarantor	Guarantor and issuer are same countries
Force majeure (yes/no)	Indication as to whether or not a syndicate may be discharged from its obligations due to certain events and adverse material changes in international, political, and economic conditions
Cross-default (guarantor)	A covenant by the issuer (guarantor) that an event of default will be deemed to have occurred in a financing if a default occurs in any of its other financing
Sinking fund (yes/no)	Indicates where there is a sinking fund in operation to provide for redemption of an issue at regular intervals
Issuer profile (-1,0,1)	Based on issuer's profile
Collaterized (yes/no)	Notion of whether or not a bond is secured by collateral (nature of the collateral is indicated in the report text)
Launch Moody's (S&P) rating	The initial Moody's (S&P) long-term debt rating assigned to a specific issue
Currency amount (principal)	The nominal value of the bond in the currency of issue
Issuer nationality	The nationality of the issuer
Presence of guarantor	Guaranteed or nonguaranteed bond
Issuer Moody's (S&P) rating	The current Moody's (S&P) long-term debt rating of the issuer
Years to maturity (maturity)	Number of years from issue until final maturity
Guarantor industry sector	The area of industry in which the guarantor of an issue operates
Issuer type	Further classification of the issuer—private or public, plus broad activity description (government, bank, utility, or corporation)
Issuer industry sector (project sector dummy)	A code field describing the principal industry in which issuer is involved
Guarantor type	Further classification of the guarantor, similar to the issuer type

Source: Euromoney Bondware definitions.

Annex D

Table D.1 Bond Issuer Characteristics Descriptive Statistics

Variable	N	Minimum	Maximum	Mean	Std. Deviation
Yield to maturity	583	0.00	64.83	8.40	4.49
Underwriting risk period	583	−8.00	7.00	0.29	0.81
Same-company guarantor	141	0.00	1.00	0.41	0.49
Force majeure	204	0.00	1.00	0.96	0.19
Cross-default issuer	222	0.00	1.00	0.87	0.33
Sinking fund	582	0.00	1.00	0.02	0.12
Issuer profile	583	−1.00	1.00	−0.11	0.60
Collateral (yes/no)	582	0.00	1.00	0.10	0.30
Moody's launch rating	176	2.00	20.00	10.43	5.67
Standard and Poors launch rating	174	3.00	20.00	11.68	5.01
Principal	583	5.00	2500.00	277.93	270.70
Presence of guarantor	583	0.00	1.00	0.24	0.43
Issuer (S&P)	392	2.00	20.00	11.08	5.98
Issuer (Moody's)	439	2.00	20.00	10.21	5.52
Maturity	580	1.00	100.00	10.26	10.50
Spread at launch	459	2.00	778.00	199.05	174.16
Logspread	459	0.69	6.66	4.86	1.02

Source: Euromoney Bondware and author's calculations.

Annex E

Table E.1 Macroeconomic Characteristics Descriptive Statistics

Indicator	Observations number	Minimum	Maximum	Mean	Standard deviation
Stocks traded, total value (% of GDP)	429	0.00	239.42	28.51	31.98
Overall budget deficit, including grants (% of GDP)	355	−16.00	5.11	−1.29	2.79
External debt (% of GNP)	222	18.36	79.40	37.31	11.53
Private nonguaranteed debt (% of external debt)	222	0.00	56.68	18.93	13.35
PPG debt service (% of central government current revenue)	191	3.19	52.84	17.57	10.16
Total debt service (% of GNP)	222	1.55	12.93	5.29	2.65
Financing from abroad (% of GDP)	257	−2.56	11.41	0.53	1.36
Gross foreign direct investment (% of GDP, PPP)	447	0.00	11.55	2.52	2.21
Current revenue, excluding grants (% of GDP)	357	11.16	50.03	23.12	9.01
Domestic financing, total (% of GDP)	257	−3.81	8.48	0.31	2.00
GDP per capita, PPP (current international $)	451	1120.00	30140.00	14581.93	7115.97
Imports of goods and services (% of GDP)	412	6.08	143.12	25.38	19.00
Inflation, consumer prices (annual %)	447	−0.09	2075.90	47.53	240.58
Ratio of official to parallel exchange rate	174	0.00	1.11	0.96	0.11
GDP growth (annual %)	451	−4.02	10.63	3.67	2.99
GDFI, private sector (% of GDP)	359	7.38	35.00	18.07	5.82
Private capital flows, total (% of GDP)	428	−10.66	12.26	1.82	4.25
State-owned enterprises, economic activity (% of GDP)	117	0.40	13.05	3.94	3.17
Claims on private sector (% of GDP)	448	8.75	208.94	83.49	56.64
Public expenditure on social security and welfare (% of GDP)	300	0.60	24.50	8.14	4.42
School enrollment, secondary (% net)	209	17.50	98.00	76.54	24.56
General government consumption (% of GDP)	412	2.98	29.83	13.86	6.54

Source: World Bank Development Indicators Database ("SIMA") and author's calculations.

Annex F

Table F.1 Macroeconomic Variables Inner Correlation Coefficients

Pearson Correlation	Log spread	Stocks traded	Overall budget	Foreign direct invest.	Current revenues	GDP per capita	Inflation	GDP growth	Private capital flows	Claims on private capital
Log spread	1.00	−0.33	0.07	−0.31	−0.35	−0.65	0.25	0.19	0.44	−0.66
Stocks traded	−0.33	1.00	0.10	0.34	0.16	0.34	−0.10	0.18	−0.21	0.45
Overall budget	0.07	0.10	1.00	−0.07	−0.16	−0.22	−0.27	0.43	0.29	−0.03
Foreign direct in.	−0.31	0.34	−0.07	1.00	0.76	0.47	−0.18	−0.10	−0.47	0.18
Current revenues	−0.35	0.16	−0.16	0.76	1.00	0.40	0.03	−0.21	−0.45	0.31
GDP per capita	−0.65	0.34	−0.22	0.47	0.40	1.00	−0.23	−0.31	−0.52	0.66
Inflation	0.25	−0.10	−0.27	−0.18	0.03	−0.23	1.00	−0.02	0.15	−0.07
GDP growth	0.19	0.18	0.43	−0.10	−0.21	−0.31	−0.02	1.00	0.29	−0.25
Private capital flows	0.44	−0.21	0.29	−0.47	−0.45	−0.52	0.15	0.29	1.00	−0.47
Claims on private capital	−0.66	0.45	−0.03	0.18	0.31	0.66	−0.07	−0.25	−0.47	1.00

Source: Author's calculations.

Annex G

Table G.1 Cluster Membership: Regulatory Risk Indicators

Regulatory risk indicator	4 Clusters	3 Clusters	2 Clusters
Economic expectations vs. realities	1	1	1
Economic planning failures	1	1	1
Political leadership	1	1	1
External conflict risk	2	2	2
Corruption in government	3	3	2
Military in politics	4	3	2
Organized religion in politics	2	2	2
Law and order tradition	4	3	2
Racial and nationality tensions	2	2	2
Political terrorism	4	3	2
Civil war	4	3	2
Political party development	3	3	2
Quality of the bureaucracy	3	3	2
Bureaucratic delays	3	3	2
Contract enforceability	3	3	2
Nationalization risk	3	3	2
Infrastructure quality	3	3	2
Corruption Perceptions Index	3	3	2

Source: Author's calculations.

Table G.2 Cluster Membership: Countries by Level of Regulatory Riskiness

Country	5 Clusters	4 Clusters	3 Clusters
1: Argentina (arg)	1	1	1
2: Austria (aus)	2	2	2
3: Brazil (bra)	1	1	1
4: Canada (can)	2	2	2
5: Chile (chl)	3	3	1
6: Columbia (col)	4	4	3
7: Costa Rica (cri)	1	1	1
8: Czech Republic (cze)	5	1	1
9: Denmark (dnk)	2	2	2
10: Ecuador (ecu)	4	4	3
11: Ireland (irl)	2	2	2
12: France (fra)	2	2	2
13: Germany (deu)	2	2	2
14: Greece (grc)	1	1	1
15: Hong Kong (hkg)	3	3	1
16: India (ind)	4	4	3
17: Israel (isr)	4	4	3
18: Japan (jpn)	2	2	2
19: Korea, Republic of (kor)	3	3	1
20: Luxembourg (lux)	2	2	2
21: Malaysia (mys)	3	3	1
22: Mexico (mex)	1	1	1
23: Netherlands (nld)	2	2	2
24: Norway (nor)	2	2	2
25: New Zealand (nzl)	2	2	2
26: Philippines (phl)	4	4	3
27: Poland (pol)	5	1	1
28: Qatar (qat)	3	3	1
29: Russia (rus)	4	4	3
30: Spain (esp)	5	1	1
31: Slovak Rep. (svk)	5	1	1
32: Sweden (swe)	2	2	2
33: Thailand (tha)	3	3	1
34: Trinidad and Tobago (tto)	4	4	3
35: United Kingdom (gbr)	2	2	2
36: Uruguay (ury)	1	3	3
37: USA (usa)	2	2	2
38: Venezuela (ven)	1	3	3

Source: Author's calculations.

Notes

1. *World Bank Development Report 1999.*

2. "Risky" country cluster: Brazil, Colombia, the Dominican Republic, Ecuador, India, Israel, the Philippines, Russia, Trinidad and Tobago, Uruguay, Venezuela.

3. "Weak" country cluster: Argentina, Chile, Costa Rica, Czech Republic, Greece, Hong Kong, the Republic of Korea, Malaysia, Mexico, Poland, Qatar, Slovak Republic, Spain, Israel, Thailand.

4. "Stable" country cluster: Austria, Canada, Denmark, France, Germany, Ireland, Japan, Luxembourg, the Netherlands, New Zealand, Norway, Sweden, the United Kingdom, the United States.

5. All dollar amounts are in constant 1998 U.S. dollars

6. *World Bank Development Report 1999.*

7. The risk premium can be measured by comparing the yield of the bond in question with the yield of a relatively riskless bond (e.g., a U.S. Treasury bond) of the same maturity.

8. Defined as a bond issued in the energy utility, oil and gas, transport, or telecommunications industrial sectors.

9. Bonds of the analysis universe were issued in the following 40 countries: Germany, Luxembourg, Ireland, Ecuador, British Virgin Islands, Denmark, Colombia, the Dominican Republic, Brazil, Poland, Russia, Argentina, the Republic of Korea, Mexico, the Philippines, India, Costa Rica, the Czech Republic, the United States, Qatar, the United Kingdom, Canada, the Netherlands, Hong Kong, Israel, Norway, Trinidad and Tobago, Slovak Republic, Greece, Cayman Islands, Venezuela, Malaysia, France, New Zealand, Chile, Japan, Austria, Sweden, Spain, and Thailand.

10. Amortization, principal, issuer name, type, sector and nationality, collateral information, coupon, guarantor information, industry and nationality, issuer type, industry and nationality, issue type and price, premium amount, S&P and Moody's issue at launch, issuer and guarantor credit ratings, spread at launch, maturity, yield to maturity, annual yield to maturity, etc.

11. The Business Environment Risk Intelligence (BERI) Business Risk Service, the Wall Street Journal Central European Economic Review, S&P Country Risk Review, EBRD Transition Report, Economic Intelligence Country Risk Service and Country Forecast, Freedom House, Gallup International 50th Anniversary Survey, World Economic Forum Global Competitiveness Survey, Heritage Foundation Economic Freedom Index, Political Economic Risk Consultancy Asia Intelligence report, Political Risk Service International Country Risk Guide, Institute Management Development World Competitiveness Yearbook, Transparency International Corruption Perceptions Index, World Bank World Development Report 1997 Survey, World Bank Country Policy, and the Institutional Assessment Database.

12. Higher values for governance risk indicators indicate greater safety from political and regulatory risks.

13. The exception concerns countries from the stable cluster in 1997–98. Deviation from trend at this time might be attributed to the economic crisis that began in the Republic of Korea and that affected virtually all countries by causing drastic fluctuations in risk premiums.

14. The average is taken due to considerations of correlation between these three variables and the desire to produce a weighted estimate of all factors. The same logic is applied to other use of average and mean statistics for estimation of aggregate cluster effects on the spread.

15. Measured by (0.0055 (interest attributed to 1 unit corruption and autocracy risk in weak cluster countries) * $7,610 million (total principal amount of countries from the weak cluster in 1997) * 12.9 (sum of average levels of such risks in the weak cluster countries) + 0.00312 (interest attributed to 1 unit of above risk in risky cluster countries) * $3,650 million (total principal amount of countries from the risky cluster in 1997) * 12.1 (sum of average levels of such risk in the risky cluster countries).

16. Jokay, Kalman, and Kopanyi, 1998, "Municipal Infrastructure Financing in Hungary: Four Cases," Processed, Hungary Subnational Development Program, The World Bank, Washington, D.C.

17. Bonds of the analysis universe were issued in the following 34 countries: Argentina(31), Austria(2),

Bermuda(2), Brazil(19), Canada(16), Chile(8), Colombia(3), Cayman Islands(4), the Czech Republic(1), Germany(1), Dominican Republic(1), Ecuador(1), Spain(3), France(4), the United Kingdom(29), Greece(1), Hong Kong(1), India (2), Ireland(1), Japan(24), the Republic ofKorea(9), Mexico(9), Malaysia(11), the Netherlands(6), Norway(8), New Zealand(2), the Philippines(14), Poland(3), Russia(1), Slovak Republic(1), Sweden(1), Thailand(2), the United States(14), Venezuela(4).

18. "Risky" cluster members: Brazil, Colombia, the Dominican Republic, Ecuador, India, Israel, the Philippines, Russia, Trinidad and Tobago, Uruguay, Venezuela.

19. "Weak" cluster members: Argentina, Chile, Costa Rica, the Czech Republic, Greece, Hong Kong, the Republic of Korea, Malaysia, Mexico, Poland, Qatar, Slovak Republic, Spain, Israel, Thailand.

20. "Stable" cluster members: Austria, Canada, Denmark, France, Germany, Ireland, Japan, Luxembourg, the Netherlands, New Zealand, Norway, Sweden, the United Kingdom, the United States.

21. Based on Gabriel, K.R, 1971, "The Biplot Graphical Display of Matrices with Application to Principal Component Analysis," *Biometrika* 58: 453–67.

22. See G.S. Maddala "Limited-dependent and qualitative variables in econometrics," 1983, p 167, p 176

23. This approach is implemented in E-Views software, which was utilized for this estimation.

24. 1986, "Longitudinal Data Using Generalized Linear Models," *Biometrika* 73(1): 13–22.

References

Ahn, C.M., and H.E. Thompson. 1989. "An Analysis of Some Aspects of Regulatory Risk and the Required Rate of Return for Public Utilities." *Journal of Regulatory Economics* 1: 241–57.

Alexander, I., C. Mayer, and H. Weeds. 1996. "Regulatory Structure and Risk at Infrastructure Firms: An International Comparison." World Bank Policy Research Working Paper 1698. Washington, D.C.

Altman, E. and A. Saunders "Credit Risk Measurement: Developments over the Last 20 Years." Journal of Banking and Finance (Netherlands); 21:1721-42. December 1997.

Appleyard, T., and J. McLaren. 1997. "The Nature of Regulatory Risk." University of Newcastle upon Tyne. Discussion Paper 97/3, Accounting and Finance.

Archer, S. 1981. "The Regulatory Effects on Cost of Capital in Electric Utilities." *Public Utilities Fortnightly* / February 26, 1981.

Bayoumi, T., and B. Eichengreen. March 1995. "Restraining Yourself: the Implications of Fiscal Rules for Economic Stabilization." International Monetary Fund Staff Papers 42.

Bergara, D., E. Mario, W. Henisz, and P. Spiller. 1998. "Political Institutions and Electric Utility Investment: A Cross-Nation Analysis." *California Management Review* 40(2): 18–35.

Bernstein, P.L. 1996. "Against the Gods: The Remarkable History of Risk." New York: John Wiley and Sons.

Black, F., and M. Scholes. 1973. "The Pricing of Options and Corporate Liabilities." *Journal of Political Economy* 81: 637–654

Borner, S., A. Brunetti, and B. Weder. 1995. "Political Credibility and Economic Development." New York: St. Martins Press.

Cantor, R., and F. Packer. October 1996. "Determinants and Impacts of Sovereign Credit Ratings." Federal Reserve Bank of New York. Economic Policy Review Paper No. 2.

Caouette J.B., Altman, E., and P. Naravanan. 1998. "Managing Credit Risk: the Next Great Financial Challenge." New York: Willey.

Chandrasekaran, P.R., and W. Dukes. 1981. "Risk Variables Affecting the Rate of Return of Public Utilities." *Public Utilities Fortnightly*, February 26.

Chermak, J.M. 1992. "Political Risk Analysis, Past and Present." *Resources Policy* (September): 167–78.

Cline, W. 1995. "International Debt Reexamined." Institute of International Economics. February

Cline, W., and K. Barnes. December 1997. "Spreads and Risk in Emerging Markets Lending." Institute of International Finance, Inc. IIF Research Papers, Paper No. 97.

Cooper, L. 1999. "The Dawn of a New Era." *Risk Magazine:* Credit Risk Special Report (October): 2–3

Dailami, M., and M. Klein. 1998. "Government Support to Private Infrastructure Projects in Emerging Markets." Policy Research Working Paper No. 1868. World Bank. Washington, D.C.

Davidson, W.N. III, and P.R. Chandy. 1983. "The Regulatory Environment for Public Utilities: Indications of the Importance of Political Process." *Financial Analysis Journal* (November–December).

Dialynas, C., and D. Edington. 1992. "Bond Yield Spreads: A Postmodern View." *Journal of Portfolio Management* 19: 68–75.

Domowitz, I., J. Glen, and A. Madhavan. 1998. "Country and Currency Risk Premia in an Emerging Market." *Journal of Financial and Quantitative Analysis* 33(2): 189–216.

Edwards, S. 1986. "The Pricing of Bonds and Bank Loans in International Markets: An Empirical Analysis of Developing Countries' Borrowing." *European Economic Review* 30: 565–589.

Eichengreen, B., and A. Mody. 1998. "What Explains Changing Spreads on Emerging Market Debt." RMC Discussion Paper Series, No. 123.

Eichengreen, B., and R. Portes. February 1989. "Dealing with Debt: The 1930s and the 1980s." Centre for Economic Policy Research Discussion Paper Series, Paper No. 2867.

Fama, F., and K. French. 1993. "Common Risk Factors in the Returns on Stocks and Bonds." *Journal of Financial Economics* 33: 3–56.

Formby, J.P., B. Mishra, and P.D. Thirstle. 1995. "Public Utility Regulation and Bond Ratings." *Public Choice* 84: 119–36.

Goldstein, M., and G. Woglom. 1991. "Market-Based Fiscal Discipline in Monetary Unions: Evidence from the U.S. Municipal Bond Market." IMF Working Paper WP/91/89. September.

Hajivassiliou, V. 1989. "Do the Secondary Markets Believe in Life after Debt?" Cowles Foundation for Research in Economics, Yale University. Discussion paper No. 911: 1–[40] (U.S.). May copies.

Hakansson, N. 1999. "The Role of a Corporate Bond Market in an Economy—and in Avoiding Crises." IBER Working Paper, June.

Institute of International Finance. 1995. "The Use and Availability of Political Risk insurance." Washington, D.C.

J.P. Morgan. 1996. "Risk Metrics: Technical Document." New York.

Jaspersen, F. 1994. "Trends in Private Investment in Developing Countries." IFC Discussion Paper 28.

Kaplow, L. 1989. "Government Relief for Risk Associated with Government Action." NBER Working Paper Series. Working paper no. 3006.

Kaufmann D., A. Kraay, and P. Zoido-Lobatón. 1997. "Aggregating Governance Indicators." World Bank Policy Research Working Paper 2195.

Keefer, P., and D. Stasavage. 1998. "When Does Delegation Improve Credibility? Central Bank Independence and the Separation of Powers." Centre for the Study of African Economics. Working paper no. WPS/98-18(U.K.): 1-22. August.

Knack, S., and P. Keefer. 1995. "Institutions and Economic Performance: Cross-Country Tests Using Alternative Institutional Measures." *Economics and Politics* 7(3): 207–227.

Kolbe, A.L., W.B. Tye, and S.C. Myers. 1993. "Regulatory Risk: Economic Principles and Applications to Natural Gas Pipelines and Other Industries." Boston: Kluwer.

Levy, B., and P. Spiller. 1994. "The Institutional Foundations of Regulatory Commitment: A Comparative Analysis of Telecommunications Regulation." *Journal of Law, Economics, and Organization* 10(2): 201–246.

Masuoka, T. 1990. "Asset and Liability Management in the Developing Countries. Modern Financial Techniques: a Primer." Policy, Research, and External Affairs Working Paper WPS 454. World Bank. Washington, D.C.

Merton, R. 1973. "An Inter-Temporal Capital Asset Pricing Model." *Econometrica* 41(5).

Navarro, P. 1983. "How Wall Street Ranks the Public Utility Commissions." *Financial Analysts Journal.* November–December.

North, D.C 1990. *Institutions, Institutional Change, and Economic Performance.* New York: Cambridge University Press.

———. 1993. "Institutions and Credible Commitment." *Journal of Institutional and Theoretical Economics* 149: 11–23.

North, D.C., and R.P. Thomas. 1973. "The Rise of the Western World: A New Economic History." Cambridge: Cambridge University Press.

North, D.C., and B.R. Weingast. 1989. "Constitutions and Commitment: The Evolution of Institutions Governing Public Choice in Seventeenth Century England." *Journal of Economic History* 49(4): 803–832.

Olson, M. 1996. "Big Bills Left on the Sidewalk: Why Some Nations are Rich and Others Poor." *Journal of Economic Perspectives* 10(2): 3–24.

Poterba, J., and K. Rueben. 1997. "State Fiscal Institutions and the U.S. Municipal Bond Market." NBER Working Paper Series No. 6237. October.

Razavi, H. 1996. "Financing Energy Projects in Emerging Economies." PennWell Publishing Company.

Roger, N. 1999. Public Policy for Private Sector Note # 196. Private Sector Development Department. Washington, D.C.: The World Bank.

Rose-Ackerman, S., and J. Rodden. 1999. "Contracting in Politically Risky Environments: International Business and the Reform of the State." Paper prepared for the Government of Italy and the World Bank Conference "Private Infrastructure for Development: Confronting Political and Regulatory Risks," Rome, September 8–10. Processed.

Sachs, J., and A. Werner. 1995. "Economic Convergence and Economic Policies." National Bureau for Economic Research Working Paper 5039.

Scherer, F.M., and D. Ross. 1990. "Industrial Market Structure and Economic Performance." 3rd ed. Boston: Houghton Mifflin.

Smith, W. 1997. *Covering Political and Regulatory Risks: Issues and Options for Private Infrastructure Arrangements.* World Bank Latin American and Caribbean Studies. Washington, D.C.: The World Bank.

————. 1997. *Utility Regulators—Roles and Responsibilities*. The World Bank Group Private Sector in Infrastructure Series. Volume II. Washington, D.C.: The World Bank.

Weingast, B.R. 1993. "Constitutions as Governance Structures: the Political Foundations of Secure Markets." *Journal of Institutional and Theoretical Economics* 149: 286–311.

————. 1995. "The Economic Role of Institutions: Market Preserving Federalism and Economic Development." *Journal of Law, Economics and Organization* 11: 1-31.

Williamson, O. 1991. "Economic Institutions: Spontaneous and Intentional Governance." *Journal of Law, Economics and Organization* 7: 159–187.

————. 1996. "The Mechanisms of Governance." New York: Oxford University Press.

Wilson, T.C. 1997. "Calculating Risk Capital." In Carol Alexander, ed., *The Handbook of Risk Management and Analysis*. New York: John Wiley and Sons.

World Bank Latin American and Caribbean Studies. 1997. *Dealing with Public Risk in Private Infrastructure*. Washington, D.C.: The World Bank.

Distributors of World Bank Group Publications

Prices and credit terms vary from country to country. Consult your local distributor before placing an order.

ARGENTINA
World Publications SA
Av. Cordoba 1877
1120 Ciudad de Buenos Aires
Tel: (54 11) 4815-8156
Fax: (54 11) 4815-8156
E-mail: wpbooks@infovia.com.ar

AUSTRALIA, FIJI, PAPUA NEW GUINEA, SOLOMON ISLANDS, VANUATU, AND SAMOA
D.A. Information Services
648 Whitehorse Road
Mitcham 3132, Victoria
Tel: (61) 3 9210 7777
Fax: (61) 3 9210 7788
E-mail: service@dadirect.com.au
URL: http://www.dadirect.com.au

AUSTRIA
Gerold and Co.
Weihburggasse 26
A-1011 Wien
Tel: (43 1) 512-47-31-0
Fax: (43 1) 512-47-31-29
URL: http://www.gerold.co/at.online

BANGLADESH
Micro Industries Development
Assistance Society (MIDAS)
House 5, Road 16
Dhanmondi R/Area
Dhaka 1209
Tel: (880 2) 326427
Fax: (880 2) 811188

BELGIUM
Jean De Lannoy
Av. du Roi 202
1060 Brussels
Tel: (32 2) 538-5169
Fax: (32 2) 538-0841

BRAZIL
Publicacões Tecnicas Internacionais
Ltda.
Rua Peixoto Gomide, 209
01409 Sao Paulo, SP.
Tel: (55 11) 259-6644
Fax: (55 11) 258-6990
E-mail: postmaster@pti.uol.br
URL: http://www.uol.br

CANADA
Renouf Publishing Co. Ltd.
5369 Canotek Road
Ottawa, Ontario K1J 9J3
Tel: (613) 745-2665
Fax: (613) 745-7660
E-mail:
order.dept@renoufbooks.com
URL: http://www.renoufbooks.com

CHINA
China Financial & Economic
Publishing House
8, Da Fo Si Dong Jie
Beijing
Tel: (86 10) 6401-7365
Fax: (86 10) 6401-7365

China Book Import Centre
P.O. Box 2825
Beijing

Chinese Corporation for Promotion
of Humanities
52, You Fang Hu Tong,
Xuan Nei Da Jie
Beijing
Tel: (86 10) 660 72 494
Fax: (86 10) 660 72 494

COLOMBIA
Infoenlace Ltda.
Carrera 6 No. 51-21
Apartado Aereo 34270
Santafé de Bogotá, D.C.
Tel: (57 1) 285-2798
Fax: (57 1) 285-2798

COTE D'IVOIRE
Center d'Edition et de Diffusion
Africaines (CEDA)
04 B.P. 541
Abidjan 04
Tel: (225) 24 6510; 24 6511
Fax: (225) 25 0567

CYPRUS
Center for Applied Research
Cyprus College
6, Diogenes Street, Engomi
P.O. Box 2006
Nicosia
Tel: (357 2) 59-0730
Fax: (357 2) 66-2051

CZECH REPUBLIC
USIS, NIS Prodejna
Havelkova 22
130 00 Prague 3
Tel: (420 2) 2423 1486
Fax: (420 2) 2423 1114
URL: http://www.nis.cz/

DENMARK
SamfundsLitteratur
Rosenoerns Allé 11
DK-1970 Frederiksberg C
Tel: (45 35) 351942
Fax: (45 35) 357822
URL: http://www.sl.cbs.dk

ECUADOR
Libri Mundi
Libreria Internacional
P.O. Box 17-01-3029
Juan Leon Mera 851
Quito
Tel: (593 2) 521-606; (593 2) 544-185
Fax: (593 2) 504-209
E-mail: librimu1@librimundi.com.ec
E-mail: librimu2@librimundi.com.ec

CODEU
Ruiz de Castilla 763, Edif. Expocolor
Primer piso, Of. #2
Quito
Tel/Fax: (593 2) 507-383; 253-091
E-mail: codeu@impsat.net.ec

EGYPT, ARAB REPUBLIC OF
Al Ahram Distribution Agency
Al Galaa Street
Cairo
Tel: (20 2) 578-6083
Fax: (20 2) 578-6833

The Middle East Observer
41, Sherif Street
Cairo
Tel: (20 2) 393-9732
Fax: (20 2) 393-9732

FINLAND
Akateeminen Kirjakauppa
P.O. Box 128
FIN-00101 Helsinki
Tel: (358 0) 121 4418
Fax: (358 0) 121-4435
E-mail: akatilaus@stockmann.fi
URL: http://www.akateeminen.com

FRANCE
Editions Eska; DBJ
48, rue Gay Lussac
75005 Paris
Tel: (33-1) 55-42-73-08
Fax: (33-1) 43-29-91-67

GERMANY
UNO-Verlag
Poppelsdorfer Allee 55
53115 Bonn
Tel: (49 228) 949020
Fax: (49 228) 217492
URL: http://www.uno-verlag.de
E-mail: unoverlag@aol.com

GHANA
Epp Books Services
P.O. Box 44
TUC
Accra
Tel: 223 21 778843
Fax: 223 21 779099

GREECE
Papasotiriou S.A.
35, Stournara Str.
106 82 Athens
Tel: (30 1) 364-1826
Fax: (30 1) 364-8254

HAITI
Culture Diffusion
5, Rue Capois
C.P. 257
Port-au-Prince
Tel: (509) 23 9260
Fax: (509) 23 4858

HONG KONG, CHINA; MACAO
Asia 2000 Ltd.
Sales & Circulation Department
302 Seabird House
22-28 Wyndham Street, Central
Hong Kong, China
Tel: (852) 2530-1409
Fax: (852) 2526-1107
E-mail: sales@asia2000.com.hk
URL: http://www.asia2000.com.hk

HUNGARY
Euro Info Service
Margitszgeti Europa Haz
H-1138 Budapest
Tel: (36 1) 350 80 24, 350 80 25
Fax: (36 1) 350 90 32
E-mail: euroinfo@mail.matav.hu

INDIA
Allied Publishers Ltd.
751 Mount Road
Madras - 600 002
Tel: (91 44) 852-3938
Fax: (91 44) 852-0649

INDONESIA
Pt. Indira Limited
Jalan Borobudur 20
P.O. Box 181
Jakarta 10320
Tel: (62 21) 390-4290
Fax: (62 21) 390-4289

IRAN
Ketab Sara Co. Publishers
Khaled Eslamboli Ave., 6th Street
Delafrooz Alley No. 8
P.O. Box 15745-733
Tehran 15117
Tel: (98 21) 8717819; 8716104
Fax: (98 21) 8712479
E-mail: ketab-sara@neda.net.ir

Kowkab Publishers
P.O. Box 19575-511
Tehran
Tel: (98 21) 258-3723
Fax: (98 21) 258-3723

IRELAND
Government Supplies Agency
Oifig an tSolathair
4-5 Harcourt Road
Dublin 2
Tel: (353 1) 661-3111
Fax: (353 1) 475-2670

ISRAEL
Yozmot Literature Ltd.
P.O. Box 56055
3 Yohanan Hasandlar Street
Tel Aviv 61560
Tel: (972 3) 5285-397
Fax: (972 3) 5285-397

R.O.Y. International
PO Box 13056
Tel Aviv 61130
Tel: (972 3) 649 9469
Fax: (972 3) 648 6039
E-mail: royil@netvision.net.il
URL: http://www.royint.co.il

Palestinian Authority/Middle East
Index Information Services
P.O.B. 19502 Jerusalem
Tel: (972 2) 6271219
Fax: (972 2) 6271634

ITALY, ALBANIA
Licosa Commissionaria Sansoni SPA
Via Duca Di Calabria, 1/1
Casella Postale 552
50125 Firenze
Tel: (39 55) 645-415
Fax: (39 55) 641-257
E-mail: licosa@ftbcc.it
URL: http://www.ftbcc.it/licosa

JAMAICA
Ian Randle Publishers Ltd.
206 Old Hope Road, Kingston 6
Tel: 876-927-2085
Fax: 876-977-0243
E-mail: irpl@colis.com

JAPAN
Eastern Book Service
3-13 Hongo 3-chome, Bunkyo-ku
Tokyo 113
Tel: (81 3) 3818-0861
Fax: (81 3) 3818-0864
E-mail: orders@svt-ebs.co.jp
URL:
http://www.bekkoame.or.jp/~svt-ebs

KENYA
Africa Book Service (E.A.) Ltd.
Quaran House, Mfangano Street
P.O. Box 45245
Nairobi
Tel: (254 2) 223 641
Fax: (254 2) 330 272

Legacy Books
Loita House
Mezzanine 1
P.O. Box 68077
Nairobi
Tel: (254) 2-330853, 221426
Fax: (254) 2-330854, 561654
E-mail: Legacy@form-net.com

KOREA, REPUBLIC OF
Dayang Books Trading Co.
International Division
783-20, Pangba Bon-Dong,
Socho-ku
Seoul
Tel: (82 2) 536-9555
Fax: (82 2) 536-0025
E-mail: seamap@chollian.net

Eulyoo Publishing Co., Ltd.
46-1, Susong-Dong
Jongro-Gu
Seoul
Tel: (82 2) 734-3515
Fax: (82 2) 732-9154

LEBANON
Librairie du Liban
P.O. Box 11-9232
Beirut
Tel: (961 9) 217 944
Fax: (961 9) 217 434
E-mail: hsayegh@librairie-du-liban.com.lb
URL: http://www.librairie-du-liban.com.lb

MALAYSIA
University of Malaya Cooperative
Bookshop, Limited
P.O. Box 1127
Jalan Pantai Baru
59700 Kuala Lumpur
Tel: (60 3) 756-5000
Fax: (60 3) 755-4424
E-mail: umkoop@tm.net.my

MEXICO
INFOTEC
Av. San Fernando No. 37
Col. Toriello Guerra
14050 Mexico, D.F.
Tel: (52 5) 624-2800
Fax: (52 5) 624-2822
E-mail: infotec@rtn.net.mx
URL: http://rtn.net.mx

Mundi-Prensa Mexico S.A. de C.V.
c/Rio Panuco, 141-Colonia
Cuauhtemoc
06500 Mexico, D.F.
Tel: (52 5) 533-5658
Fax: (52 5) 514-6799

NEPAL
Everest Media International Services
(P.) Ltd.
GPO Box 5443
Kathmandu
Tel: (977 1) 416 026
Fax: (977 1) 224 431

NETHERLANDS
De Lindeboom/Internationale
Publicaties b.v.-
P.O. Box 202, 7480 AE Haaksbergen
Tel: (31 53) 574-0004
Fax: (31 53) 572-9296
E-mail: lindeboo@worldonline.nl
URL: http://www.worldonline.nl/~lindeboo

NEW ZEALAND
EBSCO NZ Ltd.
Private Mail Bag 99914
New Market
Auckland
Tel: (64 9) 524-8119
Fax: (64 9) 524-8067

Oasis Official
P.O. Box 3627
Wellington
Tel: (64 4) 499 1551
Fax: (64 4) 499 1972
E-mail: oasis@actrix.gen.nz
URL: http://www.oasisbooks.co.nz/

NIGERIA
University Press Limited
Three Crowns Building Jericho
Private Mail Bag 5095
Ibadan
Tel: (234 22) 41-1356
Fax: (234 22) 41-2056

PAKISTAN
Mirza Book Agency
65, Shahrah-e-Quaid-e-Azam
Lahore 54000
Tel: (92 42) 735 3601
Fax: (92 42) 576 3714

Oxford University Press
5 Bangalore Town
Sharae Faisal
PO Box 13033
Karachi-75350
Tel: (92 21) 446307
Fax: (92 21) 4547640
E-mail: ouppak@TheOffice.net

Pak Book Corporation
Aziz Chambers 21, Queen's Road
Lahore
Tel: (92 42) 636 3222; 636 0885
Fax: (92 42) 636 2328
E-mail: pbc@brain.net.pk

PERU
Editorial Desarrollo SA
Apartado 3824, Ica 242 OF. 106
Lima 1
Tel: (51 14) 285380
Fax: (51 14) 286628

PHILIPPINES
International Booksource Center Inc.
1127-A Antipolo St, Barangay,
Venezuela
Makati City
Tel: (63 2) 896 6501; 6505; 6507
Fax: (63 2) 896 1741

POLAND
International Publishing Service
Ul. Piekna 31/37
00-677 Warzawa
Tel: (48 2) 628-6089
Fax: (48 2) 621-7255
E-mail: books%ips@ikp.atm.com.pl
URL:
http://www.ipscg.waw.pl/ips/export

PORTUGAL
Livraria Portugal
Apartado 2681, Rua Do Carm
o 70-74
1200 Lisbon
Tel: (1) 347-4982
Fax: (1) 347-0264

ROMANIA
Compani De Librarii Bucuresti S.A.
Str. Lipscani no. 26, sector 3
Bucharest
Tel: (40 1) 313 9645
Fax: (40 1) 312 4000

RUSSIAN FEDERATION
Isdatelstvo <Ves Mir>
9a, Kolpachniy Pereulok
Moscow 101831
Tel: (7 095) 917 87 49
Fax: (7 095) 917 92 59
ozimarin@glasnet.ru

**SINGAPORE; TAIWAN, CHINA
MYANMAR; BRUNEI**
Hemisphere Publication Services
41 Kallang Pudding Road #04-03
Golden Wheel Building
Singapore 349316
Tel: (65) 741-5166
Fax: (65) 742-9356
E-mail: ashgate@asianconnect.com

SLOVENIA
Gospodarski vestnik Publishing
Group
Dunajska cesta 5
1000 Ljubljana
Tel: (386 61) 133 83 47; 132 12 30
Fax: (386 61) 133 80 30
E-mail: repansekj@gvestnik.si

SOUTH AFRICA, BOTSWANA
For single titles:
Oxford University Press Southern
Africa
Vasco Boulevard, Goodwood
P.O. Box 12119, N1 City 7463
Cape Town
Tel: (27 21) 595 4400
Fax: (27 21) 595 4430
E-mail: oxford@oup.co.za

For subscription orders:
International Subscription Service
P.O. Box 41095
Craighall
Johannesburg 2024
Tel: (27 11) 880-1448
Fax: (27 11) 880-6248
E-mail: iss@is.co.za

SPAIN
Mundi-Prensa Libros, S.A.
Castello 37
28001 Madrid
Tel: (34 91) 4 363700
Fax: (34 91) 5 753998
E-mail: libreria@mundiprensa.es
URL: http://www.mundiprensa.com/

Mundi-Prensa Barcelona
Consell de Cent, 391
08009 Barcelona
Tel: (34 3) 488-3492
Fax: (34 3) 487-7659
E-mail: barcelona@mundiprensa.es

SRI LANKA, THE MALDIVES
Lake House Bookshop
100, Sir Chittampalam Gardiner
Mawatha
Colombo 2
Tel: (94 1) 32105
Fax: (94 1) 432104
E-mail: LHL@sri.lanka.net

SWEDEN
Wennergren-Williams AB
P. O. Box 1305
S-171 25 Solna
Tel: (46 8) 705-97-50
Fax: (46 8) 27-00-71
E-mail: mail@wwi.se

SWITZERLAND
Librairie Payot Service Institutionnel
C(tm)tes-de-Montbenon 30
1002 Lausanne
Tel: (41 21) 341-3229
Fax: (41 21) 341-3235

ADECO Van Diermen
EditionsTechniques
Ch. de Lacuez 41
CH1807 Blonay
Tel: (41 21) 943 2673
Fax: (41 21) 943 3605

THAILAND
Central Books Distribution
306 Silom Road
Bangkok 10500
Tel: (66 2) 2336930-9
Fax: (66 2) 237-8321

**TRINIDAD & TOBAGO
AND THE CARRIBBEAN**
Systematics Studies Ltd.
St. Augustine Shopping Center
Eastern Main Road, St. Augustine
Trinidad & Tobago, West Indies
Tel: (868) 645-8466
Fax: (868) 645-8467
E-mail: tobe@trinidad.net

UGANDA
Gustro Ltd.
PO Box 9997, Madhvani Building
Plot 16/4 Jinja Rd.
Kampala
Tel: (256 41) 251 467
Fax: (256 41) 251 468
E-mail: gus@swiftuganda.com

UNITED KINGDOM
Microinfo Ltd.
P.O. Box 3, Omega Park, Alton,
Hampshire GU34 2PG
England
Tel: (44 1420) 86848
Fax: (44 1420) 89889
E-mail: wbank@microinfo.co.uk
URL: http://www.microinfo.co.uk

The Stationery Office
51 Nine Elms Lane
London SW8 5DR
Tel: (44 171) 873-8400
Fax: (44 171) 873-8242
URL: http://www.the-stationery-office.co.uk/

VENEZUELA
Tecni-Ciencia Libros, S.A.
Centro Cuidad Comercial Tamanco
Nivel C2, Caracas
Tel: (58 2) 959 5547; 5035; 0016
Fax: (58 2) 959 5636

ZAMBIA
University Bookshop, University of
Zambia
Great East Road Campus
P.O. Box 32379
Lusaka
Tel: (260 1) 252 576
Fax: (260 1) 253 952

ZIMBABWE
Academic and Baobab Books (Pvt.)
Ltd.
4 Conald Road, Graniteside
P.O. Box 567
Harare
Tel: 263 4 755035
Fax: 263 4 781913